NAZISM

NAZISM

BY JAMES D. FORMAN

FRANKLIN WATTS | NEW YORK | LONDON | 1978

"This one is in honor of Forcam and its three Stalwarts;

Guy Anthony
Marcia Randall
James Douglas

In their mad battle for visual truth. May they never raise the white flag."

Library of Congress Cataloging in Publication Data

Forman, James D
  Nazism.

    Bibliography: p.
    Includes index.
    SUMMARY: Discusses the influence of nineteenth-century philosophers and World War I on the growth of Nazism and Hitler's rise to power.
    1. National socialism—History—Juvenile literature. 2. Germany—Politics and government—1918–1933—Juvenile literature. 3. Germany—Politics and government—1933–1945—Juvenile literature. [Germany—History—1918–1933. 2. Germany—History—1933–1945. 3. National socialism. 4. Hitler, Adolf, 1889–1945] I. Title.
DD253.F559   943.08   77–21184
ISBN 0–531–01473–8

CONTENTS

STAGE SETTING

THE AUTHORITARIAN STATE

At first glance Adolf Hitler's Third Reich seems as sudden and spontaneous as an earthquake or tornado. As if from nowhere in 1933 a black cloud began to rise over Europe and quickly darkened the sky. Before the storm was over twelve years later, some forty million people had died violently as a result. The map of the world had been reshaped. Adolf Hitler, the third-rate Austrian artist who rose meteorically to a position of more fearful power and dominion than that ever enjoyed by Alexander the Great, Julius Caesar, or Napoleon Bonaparte, seems himself to be inexplicable in human terms. Yet he and his Nazi regime, just as the forces that combine to generate a natural disaster, were precipitated by prior stresses and tendencies that can be traced back to their origins several hundred years earlier.

Martin Luther (1483–1546) has been called the spiritual godfather of Nazism. During Luther's time Germany was comprised of literally hundreds of small feudal principalities, and it was Luther's fiery theology that triggered a general peasants' revolt. Though he helped inspire the up-heaval, his conviction that all government is of God and that even bad rulers are God-appointed to punish the people for their sins placed Luther on the side of the princes. He approved their fearful retaliation which saw some 130,000 peasants slain with the observation, "The ass will have blows, and the people will be ruled by violence." So the strivings for freedom of the common man were rooted out in Germany at an early date and not again revived, while throughout the seventeenth century England, and in the eighteenth century France moved toward parliamentary democracy. Though Nazism cannot be tied directly to Luther, his teaching of submission to one's ruler, even when that ruler is a tyrant, preconditioned much of twentieth-century Germany to accept the Nazi regime with unquestioning and unconditional obedience.

Following Luther, Germany remained a jigsaw puzzle of numerous principalities, quarrelsome among themselves and subject to attack from every side. The nagging fear of being surrounded by potential enemies is a fact of German geography, never more tragically justified than during the Thirty Years' War beginning in 1618. Before it was over, the population of Germany had been reduced nearly by half. The dread of being hemmed in by enemies, of having to fight a war on more than one front, became a motivating force behind Prussian militarism. After participating as a common soldier in the disaster of World War I, it would become an obsession with Hitler as well, but one that in his tyrannical vanity he would fatally set aside.

Throughout the seventeenth century the North German principality of Brandenburg began growing in strength. By 1701 it had expanded sufficiently for its ruler to claim the title, King of Prussia. This occurred under Frederick I (1657–1713). His son Frederick William I, who ruled until 1740, was nicknamed the Great Drill Sergeant of the Prussian Nation. He set a tone of spartan soldiering and obedience to command which persisted as long as the Hohenzollern family of kings held the throne, and that was until the end of World War I when Hitler took up the slackened reins and rode Prussian militarism to its death.

The most influential of all these Prussian soldier-statesmen was Frederick II, known as Frederick the Great. He occupied the throne from 1740 until 1786. Frederick the Great was a hero to Hitler as he was to most Germans. Like Hitler he began as a lover of the arts. Like Hitler he lived an austere life, having more fondness for his dogs than for women with the possible exception of his mother. Like Hitler he hardened into a ruthless conqueror. Having inherited from his cruel and hated father a magnificently disciplined army, he said it was too fine an instrument to be allowed to rust. In 1740 he put his army to use, invading Austrian Silesia two days before his offer of protection in exchange for territory could reach the empress Maria Theresa. When questioned about the morality of this maneuver, he would ask how one could afford morality in a den of wolves, words that might have been spoken by Hitler two hundred years later.

With Frederick the Great's death, Prussia seemed well on the way to absorbing all of Northern Germany. While other Western European countries were nurturing democracy, here militarism remained the dominant fact of life and history. Not even Napoleon, who vanquished the Prussians at Jena in 1806, could disrupt this fierce spirit. Within seven years the seemingly moribund Prussian army had revived sufficiently to lead the War of Liberation against Napoleon.

The combined effect of Napoleon's humiliating conquest of Prussia and his subsequent eviction was several small steps toward Nazism. First, it reduced the sovereign German territories from over three hundred to thirty-nine, thus paving the way for easier unification into one strong nation. At the same time, a German tendency of the late eighteenth century to join the mainstream of Western thought was quickly cut off as an alien Napoleonic import. Conversely, with this rejection of things foreign began a resurgence of German nationalism. Whereas writers such as Johann Wolfgang von Goethe (1749–1832) had been fostering a romanticism that reacted against parental and authoritarian restraints, the reverse swing can be traced to a Berlin professor, Johann Gottlieb Fichte (1762–1814), who began his famous series of lectures, "Addresses to the German Nation: A Call for German Unity," on December 13, 1807.

Fichte's call was heard and repeated by ever louder

voices, but by none so loud in the nineteenth century as that of Otto Eduard Leopold von Bismarck (1815–98), Prussia's prime minister, who asserted on assuming office in 1862 that Germany's problems must be solved by "blood and iron," words easily transformed years later into the Hitler Youth motto, Blood and Honor. Within four years Bismarck had crushed Austria in battle and established a North German Confederation. The next four years were filled with a sense of mission; Bismarck was resolved that the German Empire must become a global power, and he thrashed France. Thereafter the current Hohenzollern, King William I, became emperor of all Germany. The *Reichstag,* or "parliament," was set up but it remained merely a democratic facade. In fact, the new German Empire was a military autocracy ruled by a Prussian king.

Enter now Emperor William II (1859–1941), the last and most dangerous of the Hohenzollern line. Without question he accepted his throne as a divine gift. Seeking guidance only from God, he dismissed even Bismarck. Always in uniform, usually with saber in hand, the emperor's portrait hung in all public offices and school rooms, and in most homes. His stern facial expression was imitated by public officials, and even the insignificant railroad station masters were obliged to stand at rigid military attention whenever the daily Berlin express roared past. This sometimes absurd and usually threatening veneer of militant patriotism was a hasty German substitute for the centuries of national tradition built up slowly in other great states such as Britain and France. Totally lacking was a confident middle class which could look back over centuries of secure and settled values. There was only the flexing of newfound muscles, which contributed to the outbreak of World War I and the disasters that followed. Only then was the stage set, the curtain ready to be pulled on the Tragedy of the Nazi Era.

PRE-NAZI MENTALITY

As the defeat by Napoleon led to a resurgence of German patriotism, so the humiliation suffered by a military-minded nation in World War I might be expected to result in a belated act of revenge upon the world. This relationship alone does not explain the peculiar nature of that revenge or why it took the form of Nazism. The Nazi ideology never was consciously created by Hitler or any one political philosopher. In this respect it differs from communism with its sacred bible written by Karl Marx. Hitler was merely the extreme expression of what many Germans had been thinking and feeling for generations, but it took his demonic energy to weave the many strands of discontent into a fabric identifiable as Nazism.

GERMAN ROMANTICISM

One seemingly benign thread in the Nazi pattern was romanticism. At its inception the romantic movement embraced all of Western civilization. But for Napoleon it might have helped bridge the gap between Germany and her neighbors. Initially romanticism advocated a return to nature and stressed the dominion of emotions over cold reason. The historian and romanticist Oswald Spengler (1880–1936) summed up its German extremes as follows: "Romanticism is characterized by a faith which is stronger than all proof." This romantic attitude would be receptive to Hitler's utopian promises and helped produce the atmosphere of mindless enthusiasm that greeted his rise to power.

Following the Napoleonic era the shared humanism of early German romanticism increasingly turned nationalistic, finding its highest expression in the operas of Richard Wagner (1813–83) which sang of Germany's mythological heroes and gods struggling against an array of monstrous and deformed enemies.

From nineteenth-century romanticism sprang the twentieth-century youth movement (*Jugendbewegung*). Beginning about the turn of the century, the youth cult began innocently enough. It was composed of nature lovers, mildly protesting against the industrial urban age. But the essentially nonviolent yearnings for utopia were ripe for Nazi plucking when the time came. Imbued with chauvinistic romanticism itself, Nazism made a strong appeal to the young with such official slogans as "Make Room, You Old Ones" and "National Socialism Is the Will of Organized Youth." Millions of trusting fanatical young Germans accepted such ideas without reflection, making the Nazi party the party of the young; they filled the ranks of the Hitler Youth program, and from the Hitler Youth graduated eagerly to the battlefields of World War II.

Larger in concept and less obvious than the contribution of romanticism to the Hitler Youth was its responsibility for the word *Volk,* or in English, "folk." *Volk* in German means more than people or nation. It suggests racial purity, nationalism, anti-Semitism, each in its own right separate but related threads of the pattern to be considered.

THE HEROIC ARYAN RACE

Take the romantic idea of a German *Volk* community, blend it with heroic music, pseudoscience, and philosophy and the result was the deadly myth of the Aryan superrace. Many cooks had a hand in the final broth. One of the first was Johann Fichte, who in addition to stressing German nationalism, emphasized Germany's spiritual mission to benefit humanity while pointing out the contrasting decadence of the French, Latin, and Jewish peoples.

Fichte never used the term race. Ironically, it originated with a French philosopher, Count Joseph Arthur de Gobineau (1817–82). In his four-volume set, *The Inequality of Human Races,* Gobineau alleged that pure races rose to prominence, mixed races declined. Most promising were the so-called Aryans, although even they seemed menaced by racial mixtures.

With no real scientific support, Germany in a Romantic daze equated itself with the Aryan. A Gobineau society thrived in that country and to add irony to irony, its most influential member was an expatriated Englishman, Houston Stewart Chamberlain (1855–1927). Born the son of an English admiral, Chamberlain was kept from following in his father's footsteps by bad health. Traveling casually in Europe, he arrived in Vienna during the year of Hitler's birth. An intended sojourn turned into a twenty-year stay which in 1899 produced his best-known work,

Foundations of the Nineteenth Century. Within its many pages, race was proclaimed the key to history. "God builds today upon the Germans alone," he announced. Jesus was not a Jew but an Aryan. The book was a sensation in Germany. Emperor William II became the author's close friend, and in time Chamberlain would assume the role of Hitler's John the Baptist. In 1923 the pair met at Bayreuth. Though considered by most at this time as little more than a political joke, Hitler was bolstered by Chamberlain's prophetic conviction: "You have mighty things to do." At Chamberlain's death in 1927 the Nazi newspaper *Völkischer Beobachter* reciprocated ominously by saying that Germany had lost "one of the great armorers whose weapons have not yet found their fullest use in our day."

Indirectly, but no less importantly, Nazi racism had yet another Englishman to thank: Charles Darwin (1809–82). Darwin's theory of evolution was based on the premise of struggle for survival among animals and plants. Man, too, was involved in this process, but was the only species that permitted its poorest specimens to reproduce. Merely an observation on Darwin's part, this was taken by some as an admonition, and the basic principle of the biological theory was quickly broadened into a wider-ranging and far less exacting statement; that of social Darwinism, which applied the basic survival struggle to the whole range of political and social life. In Germany, of course, it was given a racial slant. Pure German blood must be rescued; impure blood, primarily that of Jews and Slavs, eliminated. The concept might be dismissed as monstrous foolishness had it not been put into practice by the Nazis, and even before World War I in the nearly forgotten Herero war of 1904–1905.

Germany's first colony had been acquired in southwest Africa twenty years before. By 1904 it contained a few thousand Europeans and a number of native tribes, among them the Herero, who revolted against German dominion and killed about a hundred German soldiers and male settlers. German chief of staff, General Alfred von Schlieffen proclaimed, "The race war which has begun can be ended only by the elimination of one of the parties." Within two years the Herero population was reduced from seventy thousand to sixteen thousand. Its dazed survivors were deported to the far borders of the colony in minipreview of the "final solution" Nazism would impose in Poland and Russia.

LEBENSRAUM

If one accepted the natural supremacy of an Aryan race, if one equated Aryan with German and coincidentally happened to be a German, it was natural to further assume a priority over the good things of this earth, including space in which to thrive. Though Prussia always was disposed to conquer new territory, it took land and inhabitants together. The concept of Lebensraum ("living space") was something new. It required uninhabited land. The idea came late, being first expressed by a professor of oriental languages at Göttingen University, Paul de Lagarde (1827–91). His two-volume work German Writings, published in 1878 and 1881, reached a wide audience. Contrary to the policies of Bismarck, he advocated expansion eastward into Russia, with a new twist. German peasants were to be resettled on the Black Sea and in Asia, a goal that Heinrich Himmler reiterated during World War II: "What is unalterable is that we shall fill the area with settlers, that we shall establish a nursery garden of Germanic blood there in the East." Old-style conquest had been revised according to a Nazi law of nature that room must be made on the planet for the Aryan race. Without this Lebensraum the superior breed could not expand, would eventually become contaminated by inferior blood, and eventually decline. Territorial ambitions varied little between the two world wars. The difference lay in the brutal methods condoned by Lebensraum with its racial theories which the older imperialism could not have justified.

THE LOVE OF BATTLE

Militarism had long been a Prussian institution. Before Hitler arrived, this work of kings would be vindicated by numerous German philosophers. Succeeding Fichte at the University of Berlin was Georg Wilhelm Friedrich Hegel (1770–1831). For Hegel the individual meant nothing, the state all, and what purified and made a state grow was war, the "moral bath of steel." The historian Leopold von Ranke (1795–1886) saw Christianity as "the spirit which transforms peoples into orderly armies." Heinrich von Treitschke (1834–96), one more in the long line of militant Berlin professors, announced, "War is not only a practical necessity, it is also a theoretical necessity . . . the concept of the state implies the concept of war, for the essence of the state is power. That war should ever be banished from the world is a hope not only absurd, but profoundly immoral." Of wider international renown was Friedrich Wilhelm Nietzsche (1844–1900). He described the superman as a splendid blond brute. "Ye shall love peace as a means to new war, and the short peace more than the long."

Though the state might be reckoned more important than the sum of its human parts, the individual could not be overlooked entirely. The individual was, after all, an elemental part of the whole. The individual's value depended upon loyal service to the state by carrying out orders from above. This was the *Führerprinzip,* the "leader principle," of mindlessly following one's superior's dictates, and as such it became the basis of Hitler's most sinister and steadfast legions, the SS, whose daggers were etched Our Honor Is Loyalty. Rather than be free with the burden of responsibility for one's conduct, the sincere Nazi chose to be a machine executing orders automatically.

With a population of soldiers reared on such dangerous ideas, blind militarism reached its German zenith during World War I when the field commander General Erich Ludendorff totally eclipsed the civilian side of government.

Militarism would survive the defeat in 1918 largely because the majority of Germans refused to accept the fact that their invincible army had been vanquished. It had been sold out by the civilian government, so went the myth. So militarism survived to be used by Hitler. The führer principle he took unto himself while the military, outside the inner circle of Nazism, became a dutiful machine serving the ends of Nazism until it was destroyed.

ANTI-SEMITISM

Unique to Nazism as a political movement was the driving force of anti-Semitism. Anti-Semitism had recurred over a period of nearly two thousand years. As far as many Jews were concerned, it was a divine law set out in the Old Testament: "Just as the Lord took delight in you, prospering and increasing, so now it will be his delight to destroy and exterminate you" (Deut. 28:15). In Germany, Martin Luther was a vociferous anti-Semite, publishing a booklet in 1542 entitled *Against Jews and their Lies.* The nineteenth century endured a prejudicial resurgence culminating in the ravings of Hermann Ahlwardt, a member of the German parliament who in 1890 wrote "The War of Desperation between the Aryan people and Judaism" in which he described Jews as beasts of prey and advocated their extermination.

About the same time in France was published *The Protocols of the Elders of Zion* which purported to be the verbatim record of twenty-four secret meetings at Basel, Switzerland, during which the leaders of world Jewry planned the conquest of the world. Though an absurd forgery, even the cautious *London Times* judged it to be a valid document and a wave of anti-Semitism resulted.

The war fever leading up to World War I tended to unify the German people. Anti-Semitism momentarily subsided and Jews fought and died in the emperor's army. Defeat reversed this trend. Even before Hitler rose to prominence, Germany was casting about for scapegoats and the Jews were high on the list.

While there is no justifying anti-Semitism, or the attempted extermination of every Jew on earth, so violent a passion requires some explanation. It cannot be passed off simply as inexplicable madness on the part of an entire nation. Many factors contributed to a mood of anti-Semitism in Germany. The Nazis invented nothing new, only intensified and distorted old beliefs, and finally put their furious convictions into terrifying action.

The original justification for anti-Semitism was religious: the Jews killed Christ. This argument carried more impact during the time of Luther than it did during a more worldly twentieth century. Related to this basic accusation was the biblical claim that the Jews were a chosen people, a statement of superiority with which many insecure Christians took issue.

In modern Germany, a nation with few conspicuous minorities, the half million resident Jews prior to World War II were a distinct group and hence an easy target for prejudice. Any absorption of the community into the greater society was made less likely before and after World War I by the steady influx of impoverished and visibly shabby Jews moving from Russia and other Eastern countries. The other Germans called them *Ostjuden* ("Jews of the East") and tended to think of all Jews as international riffraff and not as long-time members of the German community.

In centuries past, German Jews had been denied the right to own land or go into farming or manufacturing, while under clerical laws money-lending and pawn-broking were forbidden to Christians. Circumstances dictated that Jews fill the vacuum, and over the years small-time financing developed into international banking. German farmers and businessmen regularly obtained loans from Jewish firms, and if a crop failed or a business went into the red, it was easier to blame the "bloodsucking Jew" than the weather or one's own lack of business judgment for the resulting foreclosure.

Jewish success within the German community was not limited to banking. Reared within the ghetto to admire higher education and hard work, a disproportionately large number succeeded to the higher professions: law and medicine. Many were drawn to the communications media: press, theater, films, music, all conspicuous and desirable occupations, which led many a plod-along German to mutter enviously that these foreigners were taking over. Jewish cosmopolitanism only aggravated this response. They seemed to thrive in the burgeoning cities and industrial centers, thereby threatening the vanishing pastoral ways so revered by the German romantic spirit. Worse, as bankers and world wanderers, Jews were identified with international interest groups which, if not downright hostile to German interests, must certainly be indifferent to them. "International Jewry," a popular term, was always vaguely suspected of participating in a wide conspiracy against Germany, and Hitler was not the first to regard them as a worldwide threat.

Nor did the Jews in Germany do very much to improve their image. They were used to prejudice; most accepted the situation and made no effort to overcome it. Many made matters worse. Treated as unwelcome guests, it was not easy to regard Germany as the beloved fatherland, and among literate and outspoken Jews such as the writer and critic Kurt Tucholsky (1890–1935), it was standard practice to denounce all things German and lampoon those traditions and institutions that Germans held sacred. As the Jews were highly literate, theirs was a loud voice, and during the liberal years between world wars their talents could have been better employed in shoring up the weak but well-intended Weimar Republic rather than contributing to its collapse.

Given this background and needing a visible scapegoat, it is easy to see why Nazism chose the Jews for its whipping boy. They were numerous and unique enough to be easily identified, important qualities when choosing an enemy. At the same time they were too few to effectively retaliate, another convenience. By singling out the Jew, all other Germans were offered by Nazism this common bond, their non-Jewishness, an appeal that worked surprisingly well in insecure and threatening times. But it would be a mistake to regard Hitler's anti-Semitism as simply a utilitarian device. It was a vital part of Nazi ideology. Hitler obviously admired the Jews. As God had his Satan, the pure Aryan must have his evil but worthy protagonist, a negative superman.

AUSTRIAN BEGINNINGS

Decline of the West

Without Adolf Hitler, Nazism is unimaginable, and its final nature was in essence his nature. He was a product of Austria developing most of his inflexible ideas in that climate before World War I.

At this time Austria had a very different socioeconomic climate than Emperor William II's strutting and self-assured nation. Here old Europe was visibly in decay. The ancient emperor Francis Joseph I sat on a crumbling throne, and the elegant life-style of Vienna's bourgeoisie had an ephemeral aura of yesterday. A minority of German-Austrians still ruled over a polyglot empire of some dozens of nationalities. In 1867 the Hungarians had won equality with the Germans under a so-called Dual Monarchy, and with the twentieth century, Czechs, Slovaks, Serbs, and Croats were clamoring for equality. The once great empire seemed to be slowly sinking. The ruling German minority felt they were being drowned by alien races and despised the old emperor for ignoring their peril. At the University of Vienna students protested wildly. Communist workers tramped in endless ranks through the city and many predicted the "cracked pot," as Austria was often called, would split apart upon the old emperor's imminent demise.

Among Austria's mixture of peoples were the Jews, many of them flocking from the East in tall hats and black caftans. Before the First World War they comprised nearly 10 percent of Vienna's population, more than any other city of Central Europe. Many retained their foreign customs and style of dress, becoming highly visible targets of anti-Semitism to a degree as yet not prevalent in Germany. Most prophetic of Austria's prewar bigots was the mystic Lanz von Liebenfels, who in 1907 raised a swastika flag over his castle. He published a hate periodical, *Ostara,* which hammered away at one theme. The Aryans must rule the world and this could happen only as the result of a death struggle with dark and lustful Jewry, representatives of which were regularly depicted in *Ostara*'s lurid illustrations as seducing fearful blond virgins.

Hitler's Beginnings

Not until he was an adolescent would Hitler plunge into the ferment of Vienna. He was born, April 20, 1889, of peasant stock in the rural town of Braunau am Inn. His father, Alois Schicklgruber, a customs official, had been born out of wedlock and given his mother's family name. There was always some question, at least in Hitler's mind, whether he might have Jewish blood, as his wayward grandmother at the time of becoming pregnant was working in a Jewish household. This concern may well have aggravated his anti-Semitism. A few years after Alois was born, his mother married into the Hitler family, but not until he was thirty-nine years old did Adolf's father change his name from Schicklgruber. It is useless but fascinating to speculate whether, had his father not done so, the burden of the name Schicklgruber would have kept Adolf an obscure and laughed-at politician.

Alois was fifty-two when his son, Adolf, was born. Alois was a hard drinker and child beater. Many Germanic fathers were strict disciplinarians and there was little love lost between this parent and child. Klara Hitler, on the other hand, was only twenty-nine at the time. She had already lost three children in their infancy and toward Adolf she was overly loving and protective. Another son, Edmund, born in 1894, died at the age of six. This and the prior deaths may well have caused Adolf to wonder, "Why me? Why did I survive?" Such miraculous preservations during his life, plus the highly religious atmosphere fostered by his mother seem to have contributed to his later conviction that he was spared by providence to achieve some divine mission.

Hitler's success was far from immediate. In 1903, the family having moved to the small city of Linz, his father fell dead at a tavern. Very soon thereafter Adolf withdrew from school "with an elemental hatred," his only positive memory being that of a history teacher, Dr. Leopold Poetsch, whose lectures gloried in the German past and the Teutonic knights of old. Out of school, Adolf was pampered by his doting mother. Fancying himself as the village dandy, he dressed elegantly, carried an ivory-tipped walking stick, and accomplished nothing. His major passion was the music of Richard Wagner. Eventually he would draw a parallel between their two lives, claiming Wagner as his only forerunner, "The greatest prophetic figure the German people has." In fact, there was valid ground for comparison. Both failed in early recognition. Both drifted for a time. Both had a fierce craving for power and the need to dominate, to put on spectacular performances. Both came from uncertain ancestry, and had failed in school. Both became vegetarian. More important, the two men glorified the heroic

German past and despised aliens. Wagner's words, "I hold the Jewish race to be the born enemy of pure humanity and everything noble in man," were music to Hitler's ears as surely as were his operas. On one occasion Hitler stumbled from the Linz opera house to climb the nearby Freinberg from whose heights, like Christ in the wilderness, he seemed to behold the world and his destiny intertwined. Thirty years later he would observe, "It began at that hour."

Perhaps, but there were doubtful times to come. Hitler had already failed the entrance exams at the Vienna Academy of Fine Arts when his mother, after months of suffering, died of cancer. Her doctor was Jewish, and though Hitler never expressed any direct animosity, he would thereafter have a horror of cancer which he often compared to the corruptive Jewish influence in the world.

Despite his rejection by the Vienna Academy, Hitler made the final move to that city in 1909 where he lived off an orphan's pension and small inheritance. A near recluse, his hours were devoted to reading and grandiose projects such as the writing of an opera or the rebuilding of Linz into the artistic citadel of the world. One of his favorite projects was to build a bridge there spanning the Danube and this youthful obsession became an adult fulfillment.

Gradually, as his funds diminished, his life-style deteriorated. He became a shabby street person, his dreams of bourgeois success giving way to the reality of his decline. He was becoming a vagrant, less than the Eastern Jews whom he observed with growing hatred. "If you cut even cautiously into such an abscess," he would write years later, "you found like a maggot in a rotting body . . . a Jew."

Though by no means a political person at this point, Hitler despised Austria's leading party, the Social Democrats, as he feared the workers, whose mass processions wound like dragons through Vienna, a vision he would recall in *Mein Kampf* and emulate with his storm troopers. His allegiance, such as it was, attached to the Pan-German Nationalist party which cried for union with Germany. One of its mottoes—"We Will Build a Germania's Cathedral without the Jews and without Rome. Heil!"—is said to have hung over his bed. Party members wore on their watch chains the figure of a hanged Jew and generally were too extreme in their opinions to attract a wide following. More effective and politically influential were the Christian Socialists, led by Vienna's mildly anti-Semitic mayor, Dr. Karl Lüger. The young Hitler regarded him as the greatest of German mayors and admired Lüger's oratorical gifts, noting later in *Mein Kampf,* "The wide masses of the people can be moved only by the power of speech."

Though later on Hitler would call himself a revolutionary, it was never so. As he sank lower in Viennese society, prowling the streets in a long shabby overcoat given to him by a compassionate Jewish old-clothes dealer, he could easily have seized upon a number of popular arguments to rationalize his own plight. He might have made common cause with the lower-class radicals and raged at the old order of things and yearned to topple the existing political and social structures. He might have marched with them under the banner of communism, but the overwhelming emotion of his formative years in Vienna and the driving force behind his whole career was fear that the old order would be changed. In short, Hitler was not a revolutionary but a reactionary against that very pressure. He never questioned the middle-class world and its values, but clung always to the hope that his artistry linked him to the better people. Everything new, be it politics or art, he suspected of being alien and apt to debase the values he held dear.

Regarding Vienna as decadent and beyond saving, Hitler would move in the spring of 1913 to Germany. He would not return except as conqueror nor would he ever forgive the city for disregarding him. In December of 1944, he refused a request for more antiaircraft guns to protect Vienna with the observation that it might do the city good to discover what it felt like to be bombed.

So, at age twenty-four, friendless, jobless, without real plans or resources, Hitler settled down in Munich while somehow retaining an undiminished confidence in himself and his destiny. It would take a world war and a crushing defeat to fill a confident German people with the fears he had known so long, but when the time came, Adolf Hitler would be there; the mirror image of the coming age.

PRELUDE: WORLD WAR I

TO WAR WITH A SONG

For generations stresses had been building between the nations of Europe. Like the barometric inequities which presage a thunderstorm many could feel it coming. In this brooding atmosphere armies went on the alert. In Munich a footloose and third-rate artist eagerly awaited the first thunderclap in the spring of 1914. Hitler was not alone. The first rumble came on June 28 when Austrian archduke Francis Ferdinand was assassinated by a fanatic at Sarajevo in Serbia. Austria decided Serbia needed to be taught a lesson. Russia supported Serbia, Germany backed up Austria. England and France fell in with Russia. Suspenseful weeks passed until Russia began mobilizing her army. It might still not have been too late had Germany not seized upon this gesture as an act of war and struck out east and west. That was on August 1. Emperor William II proclaimed in the palace square in Berlin that he would no longer recognize "parties or denominations" but "only German brothers." At last German unity seemed confirmed. Most Germans felt the war was desirable, necessary, and just.

They had little doubt that their soldiers would be home victorious by Christmas. In keeping with the romanticism of the age, the unsuspected bloodbath to follow was conceived as a process of purification. Church bells chimed in adulation. Soldiers marched away singing, the barrels of their rifles stuffed with flowers.

HITLER AND THE WAR

He had lived in Munich for over a year when the war began, though in the country of his choosing Hitler's life had changed little. He still existed alone, reading and dabbling in art. The war, when it came, was for him a blessing, bringing liberation from loneliness and the growing evidence of his artistic failings. In *Mein Kampf* he made no bones about it, writing: "To me those hours seemed like a release from the painful feelings of my youth. Even today I am not ashamed to say that overpowered by stormy enthusiasm I fell down on my knees and thanked Heaven from an overflowing heart."

He was quick to volunteer, becoming a dispatch runner, never rising above the rank of corporal because he was regarded as lacking leadership qualities. Yet Hitler's bravery was never questioned. He was wounded twice and received the Iron Cross, First Class and Second Class. While his comrades despaired of the endless war, Hitler's determination never flagged, and they began to call him the "white crow" because he seemed so strange.

Before the final defeat and his second wounding, the war taught Hitler three lessons. First, an efficient society should operate like the army, taking absolute commands from one leader at the top. It was, after all, the only society in which he had ever felt at home, and he imagined that after the war there would be a victorious Germany run by generals according to the führer principle which would become so basic to Nazism. Next, he began to appreciate the importance of waging a propaganda war. In this he regarded the Allies as far more successful, as they fixed on a few plausible points and hammered these home in an appeal to emotions, not intellect. At this technique he would become a master. Finally, he was to say later that as early as 1916 he began to realize that civilians, largely Jews, were undermining the will of the people to carry on. If this is true, he was well in advance of most other Germans in fixing the blame for defeat, what would later be called the "stab in the back."

DEFEAT

The war dragged on into 1918 with fearful casualties on both sides. In the spring, with Russia absorbed in her own communist revolution, Germany could concentrate her forces for a final win-the-war offensive in the west. It gained ground at terrible cost and without achieving important results. This was Germany's last big gamble, to win before the weary Western Allies could be infused with fresh blood from the United States, and it had failed. A counteroffensive was begun in August, and the German armies were thrown back. By September 28, 1918, the supreme field commander, General Ludendorff, experienced a failure of nerve. He called upon the civilian government to arrange an armistice.

Meanwhile, the home front, despite Hitler's claims of defeatism, had been conditioned to expect inevitable victory. For the most part, they clung to that faith. News that the government was seeking an armistice came as a shock, with the only hope remaining that the treaty worked out would be based upon the generous terms advocated by the president of the United States, Woodrow Wilson, in his much publicized Fourteen Points.

When the guns fell silent in the eleventh hour of the eleventh day of the eleventh month, it appeared to the entire world that "the war to end all wars" was over and the victory of the democratic idea was assured.

It may seem perverse to include the victors of World War I among the allies of Nazism, but that they were, even the idealistic but ailing Wilson. His first mistake was to refuse to conclude an armistice with the emperor and the imperial German generals. If this had been done, there would have been no doubt about who lost the war, but Wilson insisted on dealing only with the democratic elements in Germany's government, and in so doing stigmatized them as the defeatists willing to accept the unexpectedly harsh Treaty of Versailles.

Far from Wilson's generous Fourteen Points, the Treaty of Versailles was not negotiated but dictated, primarily by France, which had suffered the most in the war. France wanted massive reparations far beyond Germany's ability to pay. It insisted on such humiliating inclusions as Article 231, which assigned the entire moral guilt for the outbreak of the war to Germany. The very date of the treaty signing, June 28, 1919, was the fifth anniversary of Archduke Ferdinand's assassination and seemed a deliberate and cynical contrast to all of Wilson's idealistic pledges. Germany's reaction to the treaty was helpless outrage. Her armies had been disbanded. There was no hope again of taking the field. The treaty had to be swallowed, to lie an indigestible lump in Germany's stomach until Hitler coughed it up again. Had the victors aided Germany instead of bleeding her for reparations, the struggling Weimar Republic might well have flourished and Hitler would then have lived out his days as a forgotten political agitator in the beer halls of Munich.

FINDING SCAPEGOATS

The defeat, after years of punishing war, coupled with the emperor's ignominious flight to Holland, would seem sufficient to dampen Germany's spirit of militant nationalism. It never happened that way, and apart from the startling vitality and resilience of the German people, the reason relates closely to two myths, both of which were substantially untrue, and both of which aided in finding scapegoats.

The first is the so-called *Dolchstosslegende,* to the effect that the German army would have remained victorious had it not been "stabbed in the back" by civilians at home. These civilians were variously identified as the Social Democratic party, which had been obliged to accept the armistice and the Treaty of Versailles. Hitler would eventually affix them with the epithet "November criminals," who in the final analysis, like all the villains in his world, could be traced to the "international Jewish conspiracy."

The other self-serving dogma was the *Kriegsschuldlüge* (war guilt lie) which alleged that Germany bore no responsibility or guilt for the war, which was forced upon her by enemies. Germany certainly did not deserve the full blame as the treaty insisted, but to deny an eager and aggressive involvement was even further from the truth.

HITLER IN DEFEAT

On October 13, 1918, less than a month before the armistice, Hitler was overcome by mustard gas during the last battle of Ypres. While he was in the hospital, the war which he would have contested until doomsday was stolen away. He could never accept the defeat, and World War II would for Hitler simply be a second act in the ongoing drama of Germany's quest for a place in the sun. But at first he was overcome. When news reached the hospital that the House of Hohenzollern had fallen, he recalled in *Mein Kampf,* "Since the day I had stood at my mother's grave, I had not wept . . . but now I could not help it." This is revealing, for in the opinion of several psychiatrists Hitler had long identified Austria with his father, Germany with his beloved mother. Now for the second time she had been foully ravaged, and though he did not realize it in this time of mourning and growing hatred, it would be his life's work to bring about revenge.

ACT I:
THE PARTY IS BORN

POLITICAL CONFUSION

Fear and doubt were dominant emotions in postwar Germany. The old elegant and dependable order was gone. An era was over. Czarist Russia had already gone down in the bloodbath of communist revolution. Oswald Spengler had recently published his frightening *The Decline of the West,* and the old order of patriotism, divine right of kings, loyalty to father and God seemed to be yielding to nudist colonies, extreme socialism, and immorality. Most political parties were paralyzed by the situation. Only the radical left seemed able to present a program and that was a revolutionary one.

Just as the Kaiser was blamed for the war in Germany, in Bavaria Louis III of the thousand-year-old Wittelsbach dynasty became the scapegoat and even before the armistice on November 7, 1918, he fled Munich in such a panic that his car slewed off the road, becoming lodged in a potato field. In royalty's place at the head of a Bavarian "people's state," stood Kurt Eisner, tiny, gray bearded, and Jewish, a popular writer, idealist, and Social Democrat, but no practical politician. Meanwhile, in Berlin a communist group, calling itself the Spartacists, after the slave who had revolted against Rome, was urging the workers to take over the city.

The Social Democrats as well as more leftist parties made one fundamental miscalculation. Idealistically, they assumed that soldiers who had fought so long at the front shared their own horror of war. They were wrong. The conservative right clung desperately to the old spirit of Prussian militarism. While some soldiers had indeed cast off their officers and formed leftist committees, the majority, loyal to their former commanders, joined vigilante bands, called Free Corps, dedicated to withstanding the anticipated leftist terror. In Berlin that terror, such as it was, came to a head when Spartacists threatened to take over the city. Then the Free Corps veterans struck with a "Bloody Week" (Jan. 10–17, 1919), and when it was over, the workers were routed and their leaders, including "Red" Rosa Luxemburg and Karl Liebknecht, both Jewish, had been brutally murdered.

Meanwhile, in Munich, Kurt Eisner's radical form of democracy was running into difficulties from both left and right. On February 21, 1919, he had prepared a statement of resignation but before he could present it, a reactionary young cavalry officer, Count Anton Arco-Valley, shot him dead. The result was exactly what Arco-Valley should have expected. Eisner became a martyr and inspiration for a resurgence of the leftist revolution which resulted in a socialist government supported by workers and leftist "soldiers' councils."

Johannes Hoffmann briefly headed the new government, but a revolution in Hungary, led by Béla Kun, a Jew, and supported by thirty-two commissars, twenty-five of whom were Jewish—"the Jewish Mafia," according to the *London Times*— sent out waves of reaction that toppled the Hoffmann regime. Within weeks Hoffmann was trying to regain power in Munich by force. On April 13 his putsch was crushed by communist professionals led by Eugen Leviné, another Jew, from Saint Petersburg. Briefly, communism reigned supreme in Munich, but the Free Corps were gathering outside the city. By May 3, led by the Ehrhardt Brigade, whose members wore swastikaed helmets, they had entered the city. Losing sixty-eight men in the process, the Free Corps murdered their hundreds, and though Hoffmann was nominally restored, power now resided with the military, which within less than a year would set aside the facade and establish a right-wing regime.

HITLER AFTER THE WAR

When Hitler returned to Munich in November 1918, he had no evident plans and so returned to his old regimental barracks in Oberwiesenfelt, which at the time were controlled by the soldiers' councils. Keeping aloof from the political turmoil, he guarded a last handful of Russian prisoners and then devoted his days to mending gas masks. Only in May of 1919, once the Free Corps had taken over, was Hitler dragged onto the stage. Called before a military tribunal, he proved a useful informer against his former communistic army companions. From stool pigeon he graduated to the army's political department, and having proved himself a star in the propaganda section's "Civic Thinking" course, he was given the task of investigating potentially subversive political parties. One of the first to come under his scrutiny was the German Workers' party.

THE GERMAN WORKERS' PARTY

Like Hitler himself the German Workers' party was an Austrian transplant. Like Hitler it was one of several "anti" movements—that is, anti-Jew, anti-Slav, anti-Western Europe—in short, a product of the Austro-Hungarian multinational state in decline. Its original founders at the turn of the century were workers opposed to all alien influences. After World War I this original party would press for union with Germany and by 1926 would subjugate itself to Hitler's growing movement in Germany.

In 1919 the new Munich-based German Workers' party was but one of over fifty political groups in the city. Its first meeting was held January 5 in a small restaurant, the Furstenfelder Hof. Under the leadership of Anton Drexler, a former locksmith, the party's objective was to free workers from Marxist internationalism by ending class struggle and awakening the upper classes to their responsibility for the workers. The tone of the meetings was that of dreary beer-drinking complaint society lamenting the lost war, the Jews, the downfall of justice, morals, and the old order. But Drexler did bring to the group one "inspired idea," the reconciliation of socialism and nationalism, the two extremes that everywhere else seemed at odds in Germany, and this theme he put down in a dull little brochure entitled *My Political Awakening.*

Still, in January 1919 the German Workers' party was given a misleading aura of wide support when Karl Harrer, a newspaper reporter, appointed himself to the hollow post of national chairman. In fact, Harrer had anything but expansionist ideas and it would not be long before Hitler hounded him from the party.

HITLER JOINS UP

At the September 12, 1919, German Workers' party meeting a construction engineer, Gottfried Feder, was addressing a bored audience of some forty listeners on the subject, "How and by What Means Can Capitalism Be Eliminated." Sent on army business to see if the group needed to be suppressed, Hitler took no part until someone during the discussion period urged the separation of Bavaria from the rest of Germany and her union instead with Austria. This theme outraged Hitler, who had nothing but contempt for Austria, and he shouted the speaker from the room with so vituperative and scathing a performance that Drexler was brought to observe, "Man, he has a loud mouth, we can use him." To this end Drexler presented the departing and unimpressed Hitler with a copy of his booklet.

While feeding breadcrumbs to barracks mice the next morning, Hitler studied *My Political Awakening.* He liked the idea of nationalistic workers. When an unsolicited postcard arrived indicating that he had been accepted into the German Workers' party, his first inclination was to ignore it. On reflection he decided to join, becoming the seventh member of the party committee in charge of recruitment and propaganda.

That was the beginning. There is little doubt that at this time a political movement combining nationalistic and racist tendencies would have developed in Germany. Without Hitler, however, it undoubtedly would have been contained within the political system. But there happened to be that man in whom so many fears, hatreds, nostalgias of the age converged and reflected back as a mass movement, without which the second quarter of the twentieth century can no longer be imagined.

Within a month the German Workers' party was being put into higher gear by its new recruit. On October 16, 1919, he arranged for its first public meeting. One hundred and eleven people showed up. Membership began to climb and most of the additions were rough regular-army men. This changing character coupled with Hitler's increasingly volcanic style disturbed a number of the more contemplative beer-sipping workers and small tradesmen who favored recreation over political struggle. Particularly distressed was chairman Karl Harrer, who saw his small discussion circle being destroyed. With meetings drawing nearly two thousand to the Hofbrauhaus Festsaal in January of 1920, Harrer resigned in disgust.

THE PARTY MANIFESTO

"These points of ours are going to rival Luther's placard on the doors of Wittenburg," Hitler observed after working with Drexler throughout a long winter night on an official party program. This manifesto, made public on February 6, 1920, is a terrifying prediction of things to come when viewed with hindsight. Much of it is pure Hitlerism and as such is a commentary on the adamant nature of his youthful ideologies. Once espoused, they persist unchanging through his years of struggle, power, and collapse. Anti-Semitism and Darwinian nationalism remain the pillars of his faith to the death.

Of the manifesto's twenty-five points, six are specifically anti-Jewish and call for an end to Jewish rights of citizenship and worship. No other group is so excluded from the party, though the appeals are in keeping with Hitler's own instincts and go more toward the lower-middle class than the workers for whom the party was named. Nine points tend toward a nationalistic German state geared for totalitarian expansion, and the resettlement, presumably after victorious conquest, of foreign lands. All this was pure Hitler. Much of the rest came from Drexler and bore a traditionally socialistic slant; income not deriving from work to be abolished, profit sharing in large industries, and the like. As Hitler's dominance over the party grew, these proposals lost adherents through persuasion, pressure if need be, and if all else failed by way of murder and violence.

NSDAP—GROWING PAINS

After Hitler's successful presentation of the program, the party changed its name on April 1, 1920, to Nationalsozialistische Deutsche Arbeiterpartei, translating into "National Socialist German Workers' Party," with the abbreviation NSDAP. From National Socialist came the more popular short form "Nazi." The name caught on among Bavarians as it sounded like the nickname for Ignaz, which gave it a down-to-earth familiar ring.

Significantly, on the same date Adolf Hitler made his final commitment by resigning from the army. Soldiering was behind him for the time being—he would consider himself the first soldier in Germany when war came again—and art was put aside as a vocation. He blamed poison gas and its effect on his eyes for this, never lack of talent. Ahead lay the life of political struggle. From small-time street corner radical, Hitler was slowly building a reputation with night after night of tavern shouting matches, speeches, and brawls. Munich had a taste for grotesque theater, and Hitler was giving it out generously along with free sausage, pretzels, beer, and music when the party treasury could afford it. None of the dull professorial lecturing and secondhand jokes that characterized the meetings of rival parties. He had attended them and knew better.

NSDAP was rapidly becoming the political embodiment of Bavaria's legendary delight in coarse nationalism linked arm in arm with the gutter.

These qualities Hitler was to embody in physical form during the summer of 1920 by creating a strong-arm squad under the deceptive title of Gymnastic and Sports Division. The name was soon changed to SA, *Sturmabteilung* or "Storm Troopers," to match the group's actual function. Eventually the SA would become a formidable army, loyal not so much to any ideology as to its leader, but in the beginning it was only a roughneck squad designed to crush heckling opposition at the party rallies. "People need a good scare. They want to be afraid of something," and "Brutality impresses" were two of Hitler's convictions which led up to the "Battle of the Hofbrauhaus" on November 4, 1921. On this occasion a great number of hostile workers were in the audience and had fortified themselves by swilling great quantities of beer and then arming themselves with the heavy glass steins. Soon after Hitler began to speak, the steins began to fly. Though greatly outnumbered, a squad of fifty storm troopers fought back, using the legs of chairs. The battle raged for half an hour but when it was over the bloody but unbowed storm troopers had cleared the room of opposition. The rally chairman could proudly exclaim: "The meeting continues. The speaker has the floor." And so the "myth" of the storm troopers was born.

"We're Brawling Our Way to Greatness" was the SA's whimsical motto, and even when defeated, a battered storm trooper could be hauled to the speaker's platform for the audience's sadistic delight. In fact, this tactic proved so effective in winning adherents that when no bloody storm trooper was available, a makeup man set to work upon a substitute.

This was only one example of Hitler's appreciation for symbols. The most influential one appeared during the summer of 1920. That was the adaptation of the party flag and armband. Rejecting the colors of the hated Weimar Republic, he took those of the old imperial flag: a red field for the idea of blood and progress, white circle for the nationalist idea, and the black hooked cross, or swastika, to suggest the struggle toward victory of the Aryan man. Like all of Hitler's ideas none of this was new. The swastika derived from the ancient Sanskrit symbol meaning "all is all" and had been used by the Teutonic knights and several of the Free Corps units, but the combination of all these symbols was dynamic and eye-catching, and whenever possible in public view.

Party progress received an additional boost in December 1920 with the purchasing of a financially troubled racist newspaper, *Völkischer Beobachter,* which would remain the party's printed voice as long as Nazism existed.

HITLER AS STREET RADICAL

Storm troopers, rallies, flags, and slanderous newspapers, all would have been forgotten were it not for Hitler, who has been called the Marx, Lenin, Trotsky, and Stalin of Nazism. At no other time or place in history could Hitler have ascended to such heights, but in Germany, though few suspected it at the time, he was the man of destiny. The following is a partial list of those demagogical characteristics which qualified him for the role.

First, he was a man with whom other common men could identify, an unknown, unlettered soldier like so many millions of Germans at this time. He never tired of this generalization and made a point of never becoming too humanized. For the German public the details of his life remained obscure or romanticized. He was the leader, a composite image of all Germans.

As Hitler was the anonymous Everyman, so his ideas were those which millions of Germans wanted to believe. His feelings, already tested in prewar Austria, readily confirmed the nostalgias, hopes, and fears of the German public, particularly their terror of revolution from below. Fear-inspiring phrases such as "The Red Butchers" and "The bloody morass of Bolshevism" dominated the warnings of his early speeches. Anything else would have been ignored, but as it was, Hitler became the mirror in which the German people saw their own frightened faces.

Apart from these fortuitous facts of history, Hitler had qualities important to any prospective tyrant in any time or place. He had absolute confidence in his mission. He had survived when his brothers had died in infancy. He had been spared in battle while thousands had perished around him. In one of vast egomania, this was clear proof that his mission in the world was divinely sanctioned. Knowing this, no setback on the road to power discouraged him for long. Joined with this confidence was a manic and unswerving single-mindedness of purpose. His early goals never varied, nor did scruples or conscience ever stand in his way. Riot, terror, slander, murder: all were tools of necessary progress.

During these early years particularly, Hitler was unmatched by any of his rivals for sheer energy in organizing and speaking at party functions. Between November 1919 and November 1920, he directed forty-eight party rallies and was primary speaker at thirty-one.

Yet none of the above would have been sufficient without Hitler's explosive gift for oratory. Unlike ancient Greece or England, Germany had no tradition of public speaking, and no comparable orator since Martin Luther. Aided by microphone and later radio, Hitler was in a unique position to bedazzle the German public.

HITLER AS ORATOR

Hitler never entirely trusted the written word. It could be re-read, subjected to impartial analysis, and bore little of the emotional impact of speech. Therefore, he always put great stress on public rallies which "burned into the tiny miserable individual the proud belief that, insignificant worm that he is, he is still part of a great dragon." This gave that same sense of secure belonging which he had glimpsed as a lonely outsider during the workers' processions in Vienna.

His audience was primarily composed of the lower-middle class, the same as himself, and they flocked to him as to a long-awaited messiah. These masses, as he called them, were capable of absorbing only a few simple ideas, and Hitler knew exactly how to hammer them home. Wait until evening when judgment was dulled by weariness, dinner, a liter of beer. Select an auditorium that could be packed, never one too large. Fill the space with distraction: blaring bands, screaming posters, a blend of grand opera and Roman circus. Get the audience singing and shouting out *Heil* until a state of mindless excitement had been reached. All the while Hitler would be receiving reports, and only when the tumult threatened to subside from sheer exhaustion would he make his entrance, striding stiffly, eyes front, down a path of blazing spotlights between the rows of shouting, sobbing people. Silently he would ascend the stage. In the breathless and abrupt silence he would begin softly, gropingly, like a mystic, often after an unbearable pause as though awaiting divine inspiration. Slowly, painfully, the spirit of inspiration would enter him. His voice would soar metallically, hurling words from the echoing microphones. Fists clenched and unclenched, palms raised to heaven, eyes blazing, then closed, his was a performance any camp meeting evangelist could envy. And, as has been noted, Hitler did regard himself as God's emissary. Frequently he drew parallels between himself and Christ, and he was far from alone in this belief. Elisabeth Förster-Nietzsche, the philosopher's sister, said she regarded him more as a religious than a political leader, and millions of Germans normally careful and highly critical accepted all his irrational promises as they might emotionally accept holy writ.

At a less spiritual level, contemporaries liked to observe that Hitler verbally raped the crowd. If so, the crowd loved it. Indeed, Hitler frequently compared the masses to a woman, and almost always brought his speech to a sudden, violent, and, psychologically speaking, orgasmic climax, at which point he withdrew, completely exhausted, having lost as much as eight pounds from sheer exertion.

The subject matter of these performances was far less important than the performance itself. He never approached the candor of his written work, *Mein Kampf.* Verbally, he was offering not so much a social program as himself as leader personified, and ideas themselves were less important than "powerful slogans." A thinking, well-informed crowd was the last thing he wanted. What he did need, and largely obtained, was a flock of obedient, bloodthirsty sheep filled with the fear of Jewish communist wolves and ready to blindly follow its shepherd into battle.

FRIENDS AND ENEMIES

The give and take of real friendship was not part of Hitler's nature. His only enduring associations were with toadish subordinates, but he did have allies and loyal followers. The only one of sufficient stature and self-esteem to address Hitler with the familiar *Du* was a tough, bullet-battered veteran of the war, Captain Ernst Röhm. In the early days, as the real brain behind the secret military regime in Bavaria, he did more for the young party than anyone else by supplying arms, funds, and recruits. In turn Röhm was rewarded with command of the storm troopers. Hitler regarded them as the party muscle, Röhm as his private revolutionary army. In time this all too independent and socialistic bent would cause trouble, but in the early 1920s his contributions to the struggling party were indispensable.

Another early party member who did much for Hitler was Dietrich Eckart. A drug addict and drunkard, this affable and witty journalist has been called the spiritual founder of National Socialism. Before his vices got the best of him in 1923, he became Hitler's intimate adviser, giving him books to flesh out his political ideas and introducing him to friends of influence. In 1919 Eckart had foretold the ascendance of a German savior, "a champ who can endure the chatter of a machine gun." In time he identified Hitler as this man.

Julius Streicher became another ideological follower. A Nuremburg publisher, his paper, *Der Stürmer,* outdid even Hitler in the intensity of its anti-Semitism. Up the social ladder was the dashing air ace of World War I, Hermann Göring. The model of Teutonic heroism before his waistline expanded to absurd proportions, Göring lent the party an air of respectability. But of more importance at the time was Hitler's growing association with General Ludendorff, Germany's all-powerful field commander during the war. If nothing else, the relationship was a feather in the former corporal's cap, and for some time he saw himself as John the Baptist drumming up a following for Ludendorff, the coming German messiah. In fact, the days of Ludendorff's glory were over, but he would remain a useful figurehead until finally withdrawing his patronage when the relationship reached a stage of mutual disillusionment.

Hitler's enemies within the party, those who wished to cut the "would-be big shot" down to size, grouped behind the well-intending Drexler. When Hitler went north to address ι. tionalist Club in Berlin, they encouraged Drexler to in. negotiations with the unions and all other socialist righ. parties in the Munich area with a view to consolidation. Ap prised of these moves, which would have diverted the party from its single-minded course, Hitler returned to Munich. There, Drexler's executive committee demanded that Hitler justify his attitude. It was the last time they would have a chance to underestimate him. On July 11, 1921, with a grandiose gesture, he resigned from the party. Three days later he stated conditions for return, including resignation of the committee and for himself the position of "first chairman with dictatorial powers." Hitler was the party's only real weapon and the others knew it. He got what he demanded with a confused Drexler demoted to honorary chairman. That same night, at the Krone Circus, one of Munich's largest auditoriums, Hitler was hailed as *unser Führer* ("our leader"), and from this moment on, those who challenged Hitler's supremacy within the party did so at their peril. Until his demise in April 1945 he retained that dominance, allowing no person or doctrine to sway his own dictates which would be acknowledged in the public slogan, "Our leader, Guarded and Guided by Providence."

MUSSOLINI

At this time Hitler had an Italian inspiration, Benito Mussolini. Former bricklayer, schoolteacher, and socialist editor, Mussolini had experienced a turnabout in his political thinking during the war and by 1922 was threatening to take over Italy in the name of fascism, a program akin to Nazism in that it was a nationalistic reaction against communism. Apart from Mussolini's lack of anti-Semitism, the two men had much in common. Both came from modest beginnings. Both were political showmen. Both approved of violence as a means to imperial ends. The Italian counterpart of Hitler's storm troopers was Mussolini's far larger army of Blackshirts whose bullying tactics were winning over one town after another in northern Italy. Inspired by this example, Hitler fixed on October 12, 1922,

"German Day," to experiment with the same methods. Having been invited to appear with escort at the town of Coburg in Upper Bavaria, Hitler entrained for the occasion with an entourage of eight hundred storm troopers. Arrogantly they marched into town in deliberate provocation of Coburg's large left-leaning worker population. The inevitable stone-throwing, skull-busting battle ensued, with the disciplined storm troopers counting the occasion a clear victory. The next day, Sunday, Hitler's ranks had swollen to fifteen hundred strong. They again marched through the formerly hostile streets. Imperial flags hung from windows in welcome. Crowds cheered. Communist dominion had been broken. "That's typical of your bourgeois world," Hitler observed, "cowards at the moment of danger, boasters afterwards." His first emulation of Italian fascism had been a success.

Within three weeks he was again upstaged by Mussolini, who on October 28 sent his Blackshirts marching on Rome while he followed comfortably by train to take over the government. To Hitler this achievement was dazzling. Though he still lacked Mussolini's manpower, he could hardly wait to march on Berlin to overthrow the "November criminals."

1923: YEAR OF THE PUTSCH

The year 1923 would lift Hitler to new heights and then with winter, that season which he had loathed since his mother's death, it would drop him to depths from which no ordinary politician could hope to emerge. The year began auspiciously for those who regarded the Berlin government as "November criminals" and pawns of the victorious Allies. France, ever dedicated to a nearsighted policy of repression, capitalized upon Germany's inability to pay war reparations and marched her troops into the industrial Ruhr valley to extract payment by force of arms. The beleaguered German government called for passive resistance on January 11, and most of the people, grimly singing "The Watch on the Rhine," rallied behind them. Germany had not experienced such unified purpose since 1914. Nazism might have been expected to make common cause with this new nationalism, but Hitler was a shrewd gambler, who could never abide subservience to another's objective. Boldly, he withdrew party support from the nearly unanimous common front. Many of his followers were baffled by his stubborn statement, "Not 'Down with France,' but 'Down with the November Criminals,' that must be our slogan." Many withdrew from the party in disgust, but on September 26 he was vindicated. Germany was obliged to abandon all resistance and the government again humbled itself and agreed to renew reparation payments.

Besides the French, Hitler had another strong ally in 1923. That was inflation. Hitler, the former vagabond, knew all about abject poverty, loss of status, a future in which the next meal remains an uncertainty. Now all Germany was experiencing that anxiety. The value of the mark declined daily. In terms of paper money an empty bottle at night was often worth more than when it had contained milk or beer that morning. A boiled egg in 1923 cost as much as thirty million had cost ten years before. Only debtors, who could pay off their obligations in worthless paper, and profiteers, who were able to buy up real estate, gems, or antiques at absurd prices in stable foreign currency, profited. The average man saw his lifetime savings vanish. Clearly, Germany was falling apart and the government was to blame, and there in this frightening wilderness one voice was howling, promising change. More Germans than ever before began to listen.

Thanks largely to France and inflation, the Nazi party expanded rapidly. In 1923 thirty-five thousand new members took the pledge. Nearly half of these joined the storm troopers and party assets increased to 173,000 gold marks.

By the time the parties of the left were celebrating their May Day rites on the Theresienwiese, Hitler felt possessed of sufficient muscle to stifle their activities, which were rumored to anticipate a socialist coup. So the storm troopers broke into their cache of stolen weapons. Hitler donned helmet and Iron Cross. A bloody confrontation seemed inevitable until General Otto von Lossow, commander of the army in Bavaria, demanded all weapons be immediately surrendered. To strike or to submit? The storm troopers were eager to try their strength and a hope existed that in a showdown the army would side with the Nazis. Nevertheless, Hitler backed off. It was the first embarrassing reverse in three years of exhilarating progress, and he vanished for several weeks to brood at Berchtesgaden over lost opportunities. He could not afford to hold the storm troopers in check a second time.

EVE OF THE STORM

The Berlin government's abandonment of passive resistance and resumption of German reparations payments had repercussions in Bavaria. German nationalists, communists, even Hitler, who had all along mocked at passive resistance, felt obliged to denounce the change of policy. The uproar so alarmed Chancellor Gustav Stresemann that an emergency act was passed making the army commander General Hans von Seeckt a virtual dictator. In reaction, Bavarians spoke openly of secession. The ruling triumverate, Gustav von Kahr, the state commissioner, General Otto von Lossow, the commander of the army, and Colonel Hans von Seisser, head of the state police, jointly agreed that the state of emergency did not apply to Bavaria.

Secession, followed by possible union with Austria or the return of the former king of Bavaria was, of course, anathema to Hitler. He began making plans of his own. A number of rightist strong-arm groups joined together for strength into the *Deutscher Kampfbund,* meaning "German Fighting Union." Undoubtedly in the hope of dominating the combination, Hitler pledged support of the storm troops, and the very day after the emergency decree had been announced, Hitler announced fourteen simultaneous rallies for the following day. By speaking at all fourteen, he expected to whip up revolutionary sentiments to a fever pitch. Until this time the Bavarian government, nationalistic and anticommunist as it was, had tolerated the Nazis, who deviated seemingly only in their methods. Now things seemed to be getting out of hand. Gustav von Kahr, having been granted dictatorial powers in a move to counter Berlin's decree, banned all the Nazi meetings. At the same time, he so emphatically denounced the government in Berlin along with the "internationalist-Marxist-Judaic" front as to give support to the Nazis and their subservient allies. Though denied his meetings, Hitler was otherwise elated. It seemed only a matter of time until he would receive official Bavarian approval to march on Berlin, a dream that had haunted him since Mussolini's victory a year before. He is said to have seen himself at this time as Napoleon returned from Elba. Surely the army would rally to his support. If his own sense of mission was insufficient, he received encouragement from a wheelchair-bound Houston Stewart Chamberlain who wrote to Hitler after their first meeting, "With one blow you have transformed the state of my soul. That Germany, in the hour of her greatest need brings forth a Hitler, that is proof of her vitality."

Another reason for action were the storm troopers. Grown too large for beer hall brawling alone, they had been frustrated in May. Now restless and underpaid, they needed action.

October was a month of secrecy, rumor, and clandestine preparation. On the one hand, Hitler hoped that the Bavarian government would support his attack on Berlin; on the other, he feared that Kahr would initiate the attack without even calling on Hitler. Never content to run second best, on October 30 Hitler withdrew his guarantee to Kahr that he would not take action on his own. Outraged, Kahr called the various leaders of patriotic groups to conference on November 6, at which time he made it clear that he was in charge of any moves against Berlin, and that private ventures in that direction would be crushed. Hitler was not even invited to attend.

THE PUTSCH

Two days later Kahr was to speak at the Bürgerbraukeller, a beer hall in Munich. Lossow and Seisser would be present. To Hitler it seemed that the trio planned to initiate their own revolution. Not only must that be circumvented, but he imagined cornering all three, persuading them to his cause, and then marching on to Berlin with all Bavaria behind him. It was a dream that nearly came true. The meeting had been under way for half an hour. Nothing dramatic had been said until Hitler, looking like a wild-eyed waiter in ill-fitting clothes, burst into the hall, quaffed down a stein of beer, fired an attention-getting shot into the ceiling, and shouted, "The national revolution begins, the hall is surrounded by six hundred armed men." Forbidding anyone to leave, he dragged Kahr, Lossow, and Seisser to a back room, there to demand their support at gunpoint. They seemed unperturbed, even when threatened with death followed by Hitler's suicide. He was careful to point out that his gun contained the necessary four bullets. Still the three ignored him. The putsch seemed doomed.

After sending for General Ludendorff, Hitler returned to the meeting hall. "Tomorrow morning will either find Germany with a German national government or us dead!" he told them. With suggestions that Kahr, Lossow, and Seisser had already thrown in with the putsch, the audience was quick to give its support. Now Hitler could return to the difficult threesome with a two-pronged attack: the support of the audience which represented a selection of Munich's leading citizens, and the authoritative presence of General Ludendorff, who had been dragged from his home, completely unaware that the putsch was in progress. Disgruntled at thus being slighted, he nevertheless gave his support, and such was the old warlord's prestige that Kahr and the others agreed to put on a show of unity for the assembled crowd. This they did, and then with permission from Ludendorff they departed. When questioned upon the wisdom of releasing them, the general insisted they were army officers who had given their oaths of loyalty. That was enough.

As it turned out, Ludendorff was wrong. Lossow immediately met with his fellow officers, and Kahr issued a statement repudiating his pledges made at the Bürgerbraukeller as they had been forced from him at gunpoint. So, within hours, Hitler, who had anticipated a unified march on Berlin, was faced with directing a revolt against Bavaria. Torn by doubts, he vacillated. In a fit of gloom, he even offered to turn the party over to Julius Streicher. Ludendorff, on the other hand, remained firm. "We shall march," he said. In a showdown the army would not dare oppose him; and with this conviction they set out, three thousand strong, into the spitting snow of a November morning to relieve Röhm, who had taken over the war ministry and was now besieged there.

Short of admitting defeat and fleeing ignominiously to the hated Austrian border, the only recourse was to press on boldly in the hope that the people of Munich and/or the army would rally with them. But the cold had driven most of the people inside and it was not the army, but a thin cordon of police who barred their way. Ludendorff pressed on. Furious with frustration, he marched toward them and even as shots rang out, passed through their lines untouched. The exchange of gunfire lasted no more than a minute. Most of the damage was done by chips of flying cobblestones broken off by the bullets which had been fired low so as not to kill. Still, sixteen revolutionaries and three police lay dead in the streets of Munich and in minutes the putsch was over.

Hitler, his shoulder dislocated and collarbone broken from being pulled down by the weight of a mortally wounded comrade, fled the scene. He would refuse the chance to go into Austrian exile. Instead, he took refuge in a friend's country attic where he was frustrated in an attempt at suicide by his friend's formidable wife, who wrestled the gun away. Three days later, on the fifth anniversary of the armistice, he was seized by the police. The Nazi party was dissolved, its leadership dead, in jail, or in exile. By Christmas of 1923 it seemed unlikely that the world would again be troubled by National Socialism or its leader Adolf Hitler, who was refusing to touch food and had pledged to starve himself to death.

HITLER'S TRIAL: GUILTY BUT TRIUMPHANT

For the better part of two weeks, the prisoner turned a deaf ear to the encouragement of his allies to take up the cause again. In evident agreement with the *New York Times,* which wrote, "The Munich putsch definitely eliminates Hitler and his National Socialist followers," he continued to fancy suicide. In Munich he was already a martyr. A group of Swabian artists staged a living tableau at the Blute Café: "Adolf Hitler in Prison."

A curtain rose on flurries of snow, a figure hunched behind bars, face cast down while heavenly choirs sang "Silent Night." If this was not already too much, an angel came down and placed a tiny Christmas tree beside the abject prisoner, who finally looked up, revealing so convincing a face that many gullible spectators were persuaded it was Hitler in the flesh.

It took a bit longer for the real Hitler to recover his confidence. First came an appetite, then the idea for constructing a national highway system. The autobahn he would later build remains the mainstay of Germany's network of roads. Finally, when Hitler realized no ordinary humdrum trial was in the offing, he began to picture the possibilities of making a dramatic plea.

The trial for treason began February 26, 1924, before a special court sitting in the old infantry school on the Blutenburg-strasse. Among the ten defendants were Hitler and Ludendorff; among the witnesses, Kahr, Seisser, and Lossow. From the beginning Hitler seized the center stage. While the other defendants denied responsibility, he maintained from the beginning, "I alone bear responsibility." His motives, however, were patriotic. The only traitors were the criminals of 1918. With his claim of total responsibility, Hitler pushed Ludendorff aside. No longer content to be drummer for some other leader, Hitler accepted the accusation that he aspired to dictatorship and enlarged upon it:

"The man who is born to be a dictator is not compelled. He wills it. He is not driven forward, but impels himself. There is nothing immodest about this. Is it presumptuous of a man with the high brow of an intellectual to ponder through the nights till he gives the world an invention? The man who feels called to govern a people has no right to say, 'If you want me or summon me, I will cooperate.' No! It is his duty to step forward!"

With his final statement, Hitler prophesied his ultimate victory in clairvoyant terms. "The army we have trained is growing from day to day, from hour to hour. At this very time I hold to the proud hope that the hour will come when these wild bands will be formed into battalions, the battalions into regiments, the regiments into divisions, that the old cockade will be rescued from the mud, that the old banners will wave on ahead, that reconciliation will be achieved before the eternal judgment seat of God."

Despite such histrionics, the facts remained that Hitler had tried to overthrow the government, that men had died as a result, and in this light the sentence which stressed the defendant's "pure patriotic motives and honorable intentions" was absurdly lenient. Ludendorff was acquitted. Mild sentences were dealt out to all. On the basis of Hitler's Austrian citizenship, the police pressed for his deportation, but the court waived this punishment for one "who thinks and feels in such terms as Hitler." Instead, he was sentenced to five years in prison, with parole a possibility after merely six months.

"The trial," commented the *London Times,* "has at any rate proved that a plot against the constitution of the Reich is not considered a serious crime in Bavaria." Still, at the time it seemed sufficient to derail one radical's political career, and little thought was given to how the trial had borne Hitler's name for the first time beyond the borders of Bavaria, of how the foiled putsch had given the party a romantic legend and martyrs who could be ceremoniously evoked in future memorials.

ACT II: STRUGGLE FOR POLITICAL POWER, 1924–33

IN PRISON—*MEIN KAMPF*

Hitler and the others were incarcerated in the austere castle of Landsberg. Hitler took his meals at the head of a special table. A Nazi banner hung behind his back and there was talk of fast cars and opera, both of which he fancied. Following regular strolls along the castle's garden paths, he would sample the numerous food packages arriving from admirers. Hitler looked more rested and plumper than ever before.

By July he settled down to writing the first of an eventual two-volume set. He entitled it *Four and a Half Years of Struggle against Lies, Stupidity, and Cowardice,* a monstrosity which his publisher would condense the following year to *Mein Kampf (My Struggle).* Hitler kept the typewriter clattering long after official lights out by dictating to his devoted secretary, Rudolf Hess. Each Saturday he would read excerpts to his fellow inmates who gathered about, uncritical as disciples. Disorganized, repetitious and fragmented as it was, *Mein Kampf* was the most candid presentation of Hitler's ideas and intentions that the world ever received. Unfortunately, it was not taken seriously, perhaps because it began like a fairy story, "Today I consider it my good fortune that fate designated Braunau am Inn as the place of my birth," and went on, as do so many fairy stories, like a nightmare. His parents emerge only dimly in the early pages, and his own youth is characterized first as a young ringleader in neighborhood war games and later as an abused artist. For the most part, its one thousand pages are a rambling rehash of his racial view of world affairs and what he, as leader, intends to do about it. The following extracts from *Mein Kampf* are sufficient to show, in Hitler's own words, what he had in mind.

First, there was the pure but threatened Aryan race:

> The sin against the blood and the degradation of the race are the hereditary sins of this world and the end of mankind surrendering to them. . . . the result of any crossing, in brief, is always the following: (a) lowering of the standard of the higher race, (b) physical and mental regression, and with it, the beginning of a slowly but steadily progressive lingering illness. . . . all great cultures of the past perished only because the originally creative race died off through blood-poisoning.

The mastermind behind this threat, a menace of mythological proportions, was the Eternal Jew:

> This was pestilence, spiritual pestilence with which the people were infested, worse than the Black Death of former times. . . . In an infinitely sly way, he stimulates the need for social justice, dormant in every Aryan, to the point of hatred against those who have been better favored by fortune, and thus he gives the fight for the abolition of social evils a definite stamp of a view of life. He founds the Marxist theory. . . . If with the help of the Marxian creed, the Jew conquers the nations of this world, his crown will become the funeral wreath of humanity. . . . the effect of his existence resembles also that of parasites, where he appears the host people die out sooner or later. . . . By warding off the Jews I am fighting for the Lord's work.

How, then, was this danger to be combated. First, by creating a strong unified nation responsive to the dictates of one leader. "We realized as early as 1919 that the new movement has to carry out, first, as its highest aim, the nationalization of the masses. . . . The stronger has to rule and he is not to amalgamate with the weaker one, that he may not sacrifice his own greatness." In anticipation of a euthanasia program he added, "He who is not physically and mentally healthy and worthy must not perpetuate his misery in the body of his child." To give structure to the whole was his *Führerprinzip* ("leader principle"): "The principle which once made the Prussian army the most marvelous instrument of the German people has to be some day in a transformed meaning the principle of the construction of our whole state constitution, authority of every leader towards below and responsibility towards above." As far as the party, and eventually the nation were concerned, Hitler would adhere to this idea: one nation duty-bound to follow its leader's decisions. And in Hitler's case, those decisions meant conquest:

> Marxism itself plans to transmit the world systematically into the hands of Jewry. In opposition to this the "Folkish" view recognizes the importance of mankind in its racially innate elements. In principle, it seems in the state only a means to an end, and as its end it considers the preservation of the racial existence of men. . . . German Austria must return to the great German motherland. . . . common blood belongs in a common Reich.

Extending this concept conceivably to include Czechoslovakia and parts of Poland, he added, "Pressed countries will not be brought back into the bosom of a common Reich by means of fiery protests, but by a mighty sword. . . . the goal of a German foreign policy of today must be the preparation of the reconquest of freedom for tomorrow."

The immorality of initiating unprovoked war never was a problem for Hitler. It wasn't even a relevant question, for in his view nature was a struggle and a man's or nation's right to survive was proved by his ability to do so at the expense of others: "He who wants to live should fight, therefore, and he who does not want to battle in this world of eternal struggle does not deserve to be alive."

Once the Aryans of Austria, Czechoslovakia, and Poland were returned to the Reich, the next step was to turn on the rest of the world: "We must at last become entirely clear about this; The German people's irreconcilable mortal enemy is and remains France." For Hitler France was not a goal for his *Lebensraum* plan, but simply an inevitable foe which had to be dealt with before he could have a free hand in the east. At this time Hitler admired Great Britain. More Aryan than most, Great Britain was imagined as a future ally, mistress of the seas which Hitler loathed, while Germany would be supreme on the continent of Europe.

With France defeated and England disinterested, Hitler could turn to his final goal, living space for the pure Aryan race free of Marxist-Jewish contamination:

> The foreign policy of a Folkish state is charged with
> guaranteeing the existence on this planet of the race
> embraced by the state, by establishing between the
> number and growth of the population on the one hand,
> and the size and value of the soil and territory, on the
> other hand, a viable, natural relationship. . . . We terminate
> the endless German drive to the south and west of Europe
> and direct our gaze towards the lands in the East. We
> finally terminate the colonial and trade policy of the
> pre-war period, and proceed to the territorial policy of the
> future. . . . If one wanted land and soil in Europe, then,
> by and large this could only have been done at Russia's
> expense. And then the New Reich would again have to start
> marching along the road of the knights of former times to
> give, with the help of the German sword, the soil to the
> plow and the daily bread to the nation.

Hitler's ruthless plan for the future of the world was all there in the two volumes of *Mein Kampf.* Ten thousand copies sold in 1925, less after that until Hitler came to power, when it took its place beside the Bible in many German homes. It was not translated into English until 1938, and of those who read it, few recognized it as a candid statement of concrete policies Hitler intended to carry out. Even when Hitler became dictator nearly a decade later, few could believe that he would not modify such adolescent notions, but then few regarded Hitler as the eternal adolescent, which subsequent psychiatric study has shown to be the case; unswerving, impervious to doubt, ready to turn early prejudices and hatreds into ruthless action.

THE PARTY IN HITLER'S ABSENCE

His months in jail were a period of relaxation and reappraisal for Hitler. Removed from party affairs on the outside, it came as a satisfaction to see the squabbling of his leaderless followers unable to agree upon who should act as his deputy. The last thing Hitler wanted was the emergence of a competent rival or coalition of rivals taking over. Throughout his tyrannical career he characteristically encouraged quarrels between his subordinates. When one or another came to him asking for support or guidance, he would simply demand privacy for his writing. Leaderless, the party split widened, some trying to imagine what Hitler wanted done, others, disillusioned with National Socialism, establishing their own parties. Ludendorff, who had never regarded himself as subservient to Hitler, headed a new National Socialist German Freedom party and in the 1924 elections polled two million votes. The general claimed credit for this minor victory while Hitler smoldered. The party over which Hitler still reigned supreme was falling apart. Had Hitler served out his full term, the collapse might have been permanent, but on December 20, 1924, as the prisoners in Landsberg Castle were making ready for Christmas, a telegram arrived ordering Hitler's release.

THE LEAN YEARS

Hitler emerged from prison with the same convictions as when he had entered. Only the means to those ends had changed. As he had remarked at his trial, "The hour will come when the *Reichswehr* [army] will be on our side." The storm troopers, he had concluded, would never be a match for a heavily armed *Reichswehr.* In future it would be given a subsidiary role. Coincidentally, the emphasis would shift from street fighting—behaving "like a natural force" as Hitler phrased it—and focus on playing politics within the limits of the constitution. Only when power was obtained by legitimate means would the party take over and apply itself and the nation to Hitler's fixed objectives.

Though little over a year had passed since Hitler had been removed from the public scene, times had changed drastically. They no longer favored violent ways. Germany had been desperate in 1923 and had been responsive to violent deeds, but the volley of shots that had rung out in the streets of Munich on November 8, 1923, had sounded a call to order. The postwar period was over. Nazism, which had thrived on the nation's misfortunes, now seemed about to fall from the vine. France had awakened to the futility of her Ruhr policy and under the ministrations of a financial expert, Hjalmar Horace Greeley Schacht, a new mark was being issued, and with the influx of American capital Germany's economy was well on the way to recovery. The Weimar Republic gave promise of becoming a lasting success.

Hitler's movement, on the other hand, was in disarray. With his lieutenants at odds, dead, or in exile, membership had fallen to about seven hundred. Viewed objectively, National Socialism's prospects were nil. Despite Hitler's performance at the trial, it had been forgotten over the intervening months. The army and most of the private patrons had withdrawn their support. Another man might have been discouraged. Not Hitler; he saw a future rich in promise and he knew how to wait and use his time. Perhaps he sensed great sociological changes; industrialization and urbanization which were disrupting the lower-middle class from whence his firmest support had come and would come again. More likely he depended on the "communist-Jewish conspiracy" to throw a monkey wrench into the Weimar machinery.

Whatever Hitler expected, his own first steps were inauspicious. On February 16, 1925, the Bavarian government canceled its state of emergency and removed its restrictions on NSDAP. Eleven days later Hitler made the mistake of reentering public life where the putsch had begun, at the Bürgerbraukeller. "It is my wish that the swastika flag shall be my shroud if next time the struggle lays me low," he told the audience, and concluded with the refrain, "To this struggle of ours there are only two possible issues, either the enemy passes over our bodies or we pass over theirs!" This was too sudden and too provocative for the authorities. Hitler was fobidden to speak publicly in Bavaria for two years and the ban spread quickly throughout most of Germany.

RÖHM AND THE STRASSERS

The Nazi party had been functioning, after a fashion, for over a year without Hitler and it still had a few members of independent spirit who clung to the conviction that National Socialism implied socialism in the traditional sense, as indicated in the party's original manifesto. A free spirit from the beginning, Ernst Röhm regarded his storm troopers as a revolutionary army, and in April of 1925 he demanded they be separated, under his command, from the National Socialist party. Hitler, who regarded the storm troopers as no more than the party muscle, exploded. Röhm walked out in a huff and the following day presented his written resignation. Hitler had used this trick himself, and as head of the SA, Röhm fully expected that it would be refused due to his indispensability. Hitler, however, kept silent, and a deflated Röhm accepted an invitation from South America to join the Bolivian army as a lieutenant colonel. Five years later he would return to assume his old position with the same old ideas, a combination that in time would trigger a bloody reckoning, but for the moment the storm troopers ceased being a problem for Hitler.

While Hitler was imprisoned, a younger champion had been rising in the party ranks: Gregor Strasser, talented speaker and firm believer in socialism. To persuade Strasser to abandon the newly founded National Socialist German Freedom movement, Hitler named him Nazi party leader in North Germany. Hitler must have known this was risky, for Strasser had his own ideas, leadership talent, and the confidence of the political opposition which Hitler lacked. Many Nazis hoped he would eventually take Hitler's place.

Upon assuming his post in the north, Strasser took as his assistant a bright young Rhinelander with a clubfoot. The Poison Dwarf, as he would come to be called, Paul Joseph Goebbels initially supported Strasser's form of socialism wholeheartedly. He went further, sympathizing with communism, and entertained the naïve hope that he might persuade Hitler that the only difference between Nazism and communism was the latter's attachment to an international movement; Nazism, of course, was adamantly national.

The growing northern deviation began to display itself in the committee organized in Hagen on September 10, 1925. There was talk of a counterattack against the ossified bigwigs in Munich, and Strasser had the temerity to call for combination with Moscow against "French militarism, British imperialism and Wall Street capitalism." Even worse, he summoned the party to repudiate its cowardly submission to legality and seize power by direct assault; the "politics of cataclysm," he called it.

This was too much for Hitler. On February 14, 1926, he convoked a leadership meeting at Bamberg. Strasser and Goebbels were among the few northern leaders able to make the long, inconvenient trip, so from the first the assembly was stacked in Hitler's favor. When the time came, he did not attack his two rivals directly. He simply resorted to the old trick. They must accept him as absolute leader or expect his resignation. This ploy had failed with Röhm, but the question was asked this time of loyal southern Nazis who sensed that without their leader the party would fall apart. As a result, Strasser was easily repudiated and what might have been a new political path or schism for Nazism became but an annoying deviation. Hitler was confirmed. As one supporter characterized it, "Our program can be expressed in two words, 'Adolf Hitler.' "

It was not quite that simple. Gregor Strasser was not entirely repentant, though his secretary, Goebbels, a real hero-worshiper, after a period of despair attached his loyalty to Hitler, a fanatical devotion which he would maintain to the death. Sensing this, Hitler set Goebbels up as the party *Gauleiter* ("district leader") in Berlin, a post that unavoidably turned him into Strasser's rival in the north. There, despite strong communist opposition, Goebbels, himself an able speaker and propaganda expert, made rapid progress in obtaining party recruits. Perhaps his most memorable achievement was the deification of a nondescript storm trooper, Horst Wessel. Before being found and killed by a rival in a prostitute's apartment, Wessel had composed a poem, "Raise High the Flag." When the jealous lover turned out to be a communist, Goebbels elevated Wessel's funeral into a near Roman triumph. The poem was set to music. In time it would become the party anthem. All along the parade route storm troopers battled with communist workers, and at the graveside Goebbels called out the roll. When he reached the name "Horst Wessel?" the storm troopers boomed back in menacing chorus, "Present!"

It was corny but effective propaganda. Still, it did not entirely overshadow the lingering Strasser problem. If Gregor was publicly chastened, his younger brother Otto was not. Otto was the leading editorial writer for three newspapers established by Gregor. Until 1930 he kept jabbing away at Hitler, until Gregor felt obliged to publicly disassociate himself from his brother's views by resigning his own editorship. That was July 1, 1930. Three days later the newspapers accounted, "The Socialists are leaving NSDAP." Such dramatic words produced pitiful results. Only two dozen former Nazis followed Otto into what was to be total obscurity, an obscurity that did much to hamper Gregor's diminishing authority. He was given one last chance two years later, when Chancellor Kurt von Schleicher would invite him to become vice-chancellor and minister president of Prussia. It was a golden opportunity for Gregor Strasser to derail Hitler, but if nothing else he was loyal to Hitler and asked the latter's approval. Hitler correctly saw the invitation as an attempt to divide the party and pressured Strasser's resignation. Thus the trail ended for the "socialism" in National Socialism except as Hitler defined it. According to Hitler's definition, it had nothing to do with economics but implied the responsibility of the nation for the individual, while nationalism, conversely, was the dedication of the individual to the nation. This was a dubious definition, to be sure, but no political opposition remained to question it.

THE STATE WITHIN A STATE

After the Bamberg meeting Hitler would remain the only party member indisputably known as the führer. Having re-established his own dominion, he would set about shaping the party into a versatile instrument for his political ambitions.

Twenty-four hundred party demonstrations in 1925 had done little to attract public interest. The Berlin government continued to make progress at stabilizing the economy and Hitler was officially silenced. His only recourse was to work within the party structure itself, however meager, fashioning a replica in miniature of German society. First, he needed a centralized command structure under his leadership. Then, in mimicry of the national government, a full-fledged bureaucracy was sketched out, with all the numerous departments for foreign policy, defense, and justice paralleling the state bureaucracy. By the time National Socialism took over in 1933, Goebbels could assert that "it need only transfer its organization, and intellectual and spiritual principles to the state, for the 'state within a state' already existed and had anticipated every contingency."

Most awesome and portentous of all the departments of the Nazi bureaucracy formed during the 1920s was the SS, or Schutzstaffel. They began as a small elite personal bodyguard to Hitler. In 1926 the storm troopers had adopted a new uniform featuring brown shirts, originally intended for German troops in the East Africa colony which had been forfeited to England as part of the World War I settlement. The color of the fabric which had been purchased wholesale led to the Storm Troopers' nickname, "Brownshirts." So the SS chose for their uniform the more elegant and ominous black. In 1929 they numbered a modest 280. Then in 1929 a former schoolmaster, Heinrich Himmler, took command, swelling the black-clad ranks to a quarter million within five years. More than a personal bodyguard at this point, the SS thought of itself as an elite Aryan force dedicated to protecting the racial purity of Germany. To this end they would perpetrate most of the crimes against humanity for which Hitler's Third Reich was responsible.

Apart from purging heretics and organizing the party against the occasion of its accession to power, an event that Hitler awaited with untroubled conviction, he devoted himself to the publication of the second volume of *Mein Kampf.* In it he sharpened his political philosophy and, once the ban on speechmaking was lifted on March 5, 1927, he told the German public what it ought to believe.

The second volume of *Mein Kampf* appeared in the late autumn of 1926; its most important contribution was to show Hitler's imperial dreams shifting away from France and the West toward Russia and the East. With his right to speak publicly restored, Hitler would exercise it fifty-six times in 1927, an outpouring that diminished thereafter to only twenty-nine such appearances in 1929. Circumstances remained unfavorable; his image seemed better served by a semidivine withdrawal to the cloudy mountain fastness of Berchtesgaden. Here he could ponder his multifaceted obsession: Aryanism–*Lebensraum*–"Jewish threat." Hitler continued to meld them into a single doctrine. Germany, if it did not gain living space by force of arms, would fall victim to the Jewish enemy. The elements had all been there before but never in such an inseparable bond. Time was running out. He must conquer territory in the east, provide *Lebensraum,* eliminate the Jew, or Germany was lost.

So Hitler waited out the lean years, impatient yet confident that his time was ordained. Buoyed up by this conviction, the party, too, proved that even if it could not win the day against adverse circumstances, it could endure on its own.

THE GOD-SENT DEPRESSION

The inflation of the early 1920s had carried Hitler near to victory. After receiving less than 3 percent of the votes in the national Reichstag elections of 1928, it was clear that Hitler's only hope was another national disaster to prove that he had been right all along about the uselessness of the Weimar government. Unfortunately for Hitler, the Weimar government was doing very well behind the efforts of Gustav Stresemann. In 1919, as head of the People's party, Stresemann had been regarded as a mouthpiece for the supreme command, "Ludendorff's young man." Through the bad years he had walked a tightrope between dissent from right and left and by 1924 was achieving tranquillity in Germany and reconciliation with the Allies. As foreign minister he had reduced reparations and brought Germany into the League of Nations. Then, when all seemed well, worn out by his unceasing efforts, he suddenly died on October 3, 1929. That was the first of a one-two punch to German stability which Hitler had been anticipating. Already there were hints of trouble to come.

Throughout 1929 unemployment was on the rise in Germany. Three million were out of work; businesses were beginning to fail at an alarming rate. Then, exactly three weeks after Stresemann's death, came the Wall Street Stock Market crash which reverberated around the world. The Great Depression was on. The shaky German prosperity, which counted on foreign loans, especially from the United States, and upon world trade, saw the loans come to a jolting halt and the international markets dry up as well. Like falling dominoes the German economy plummeted; stock prices fell, factories shut down, jobs were lost, mortgages foreclosed, and worst of all, a mood of hopelessness engulfed the entire society. Defeat, political turmoil, inflation had left Germany with a residue of pessimism unknown in most other economically stricken countries. There had to be a way out, and of course there was: Hitler's way.

As early as February 2, 1930, Hitler could forecast with absolute conviction that "the triumph of our program will happen . . . at the outside within two and a half to three years." It seemed almost inevitable. The new coalition government disintegrated under the first pressures of the depression in the spring of 1930. While the elections of 1928 had sent only 12 Nazis to the Reichstag parliament, September elections in 1930 saw the number increase to 107. The communists also made dramatic gains and the moderate, democratic center was menaced from right and left.

NAZI APPEALS

Nazi pledges were the same as they had always been but the setting had altered drastically. Germany was in a state of crisis and disillusionment. The sinking middle class was terrified by the prospect of losing identity and status. From below they felt threatened by the communists, from above abandoned by capitalism. The Weimar Republic had failed and Hitler was there to say I told you so. He rejected the communist proletariat, promised to control the capitalists and restore Germany, old nostalgic glories were pasted on a cloud-cuckoo land future. The lower-middle class listened and heard resurrection and security guaranteed by a powerful state.

Nazism offered attractions for most other groups in Germany. The class-conscious proletariat had always opposed Nazism, but the promise of jobs began to erode this solid front as joblessness spread. The prospect of a revived military defense program attracted business, which envisioned prosperous government contracts, and it appealed to the armed forces which had lived for so long in obscurity. A special effort was made regarding the young people who would be the recipients of this glowing future state. A Hitler Youth program was already training volunteers. In fact, with the jingoistic mentality of Nazism stressing race rather than class, all Germans, with the pointed exception of Jews, had a place and automatic status. They were better than Jews, and it is sociological fact that when a group of people have lost their self-esteem, there is nothing more reassuring than to feel superior to someone else.

1930

From the inception of the depression in 1929, the battle for power would go on for just over three years, years of furious campaigning, street brawling, and elections as one chancellor after another failed to achieve support in a divided Reichstag.

On March 28, 1930, Heinrich Brüning had taken over as

chancellor of the Reichstag, but with ten political parties all polling over a million votes, he was unable to assemble a workable coalition. New Reichstag elections were scheduled for September 14 and Hitler sensed the time had come to strike hard.

As main organizer and star performer, Hitler campaigned with an omnibus program, making twenty speeches during the last six weeks before election. Tirelessly he traveled to every corner of Germany by train, car, and plane. No economist, lacking any theory concerning the depression or how to combat it, he named those who had thrust it upon the innocent German people. The villains were the usual—Marxists, Jews, jealous Allies, corrupt politicians of Weimar—and crowds of the distressed came out to hear him tell all about it.

However unlikely it may sound, Hitler had no greater ally than the communists. Never, even when it was too late, would they throw in with Hitler's other opponents to form an anti-Nazi coalition. This blind spot was, in large part, thanks to Soviet doctrine which held that National Socialism was merely the final plateau before the downfall of capitalism. As naturally as a spring bud Nazism would flower into communism. Such was the theory on one hand; but in actuality there were street battles between the storm troopers and the less theoretical Red workers, and their bloody contests increasingly created the atmosphere of "silent civil war" which with its terrors and brutality forced more moderate Germans to align themselves with one side or the other. The majority chose Nazism with its nationalistic appeal.

September 14, 1930, was the day of reckoning and it signaled a sad turning point in the short history of the Weimar Republic. Toward dawn of the following day votes were tallied and NSDAP, which had polled only 810,000 votes in the preceding election, had inflated its popularity to 6.5 million. From 12 Reichstag seats it increased its membership to 107; from a position of relative obscurity its representative strength was suddenly second only to the Social Democratic membership. This was a great victory but no final one; with unflagging determination Hitler carried his quest for power into a year of deepening depression, 1931.

1931

For the Nazis, 1931 was a year of consolidating gains and building up the SA into a massive army. Even without Röhm, there had remained great dissatisfaction among the storm troopers over the drift away from true socialism. This was heightened by an increasingly meager payroll; it came to a crisis when the SA commander Pfeffer von Salomon resigned after having his demand for a strengthened SA refused. At first Hitler announced that he would command the Brownshirts personally. That was his usual pattern, but the times were too demanding. On January 4 he announced the return of Captain Röhm from Bolivia's war against Paraguay. With a pledge from Hitler of a free hand, Röhm was back at his old post. Thanks to his organizational talents, within two years his private army would swell to over half a million men, well equipped to carry out a successful head-banging campaign against the communist street fighters.

For the average German, 1931 was more horrendous than the year before. Five million wage earners were unemployed. They cursed the bosses. Mortgages had time to ripen upon shops, homes, and farms. Upon eviction the former owners blamed the big "Jewish" department store owners and the "Jewish" bankers. Meanwhile, the divided parliament floundered helplessly and aging President Paul von Hindenburg relaxed into senility. Frustrated university students looking forward to a hopeless future paraded outside the Reichstag to˙ protest their incompetent politicians. Only the Nazis worked hard with clear purpose and rejoiced, ever more certain that their hour was at hand.

1932

Hitler's growing success coupled with the failures of the government to form a coalition inevitably led to the question: should he be appointed chancellor? The job was obtained by way of presidential appointment; as early as October 14, 1931, the Nazi leader had been ushered into President von Hindenburg's presence with this possibility in mind. That meeting did not go well. The old field marshal's thunderous basso voice and towering six-and-a-half-foot frame cowed Hitler and left Hindenburg with the impression that Hitler might rise as high as head of the Postal Department but certainly no higher.

Hitler had other ideas. A presidential election was due on March 13, 1932. Not until mid-February did Hindenburg announce his candidacy. Though Hitler's intentions were not made public until Feburary 27, his unsuccessful audience with Hindenburg had helped make up his mind in January. On the seventeenth of that month he revealed an expedient trend in his thinking when he addressed the Industry Club in Düsseldorf. If a campaign were to be mounted, funds would be necessary, and funds in abundance could only be had from the rich; so for this group of still-skeptical industrialists, he pledged to suppress the unions while putting forward national public works projects and rearmament under the management of the businessmen to whom he spoke. All this bounty he contrasted with the horror of communist takeover; when he was finished, many listeners were ready to make substantial contributions.

A technicality concerning his running for public office was Hitler's lack of German citizenship. He was still officially an Austrian, but this was easily resolved by the absurd device of having the Nazi Minister of the Interior for the State of Brunswick name Hitler an attaché of the Brunswick Legation in Berlin, from which citizenship followed automatically. He was now off and running. Throughout the brief campaign President Hindenburg appeared but once, just before the election. At that time he indicated he had placed his name in competition only for those who had urged him in the hope of forestalling victory of either the radical left or reactionary right. In contrast to this negativism Hitler made at least one major speech each day, more often three, in which he scourged the masses with the fear of Germany's ruin, blamed the government for thirteen years of disaster, and mouthed the old symbols of honor, fatherland, German destiny. Behind him were 800,000 steadfast party members, untold millions of voters, primarily the little people to whom he was more closely attuned than were the business leaders, or Chancellor Brüning whose response to the unremitting depression was to grimly keep tightening the belt. Surely, Hitler told them, it was time for a change, time for "the old gentleman," as he referred to Hindenburg, to retire.

With such high hopes the election results came as a shock. Hindenburg won 49.6 percent of the votes, Hitler only 30 percent, with the remainder scattered among lesser candidates. For the first time since the putsch, Hitler had been set back and both sides knew it. An unrepentant Otto Strasser printed up street posters casting Hitler as Napoleon retreating from Moscow; a downcast Goebbels admitted, "The dream of power was temporarily over."

Since Hindenburg was 0.5 percent short of an absolute majority, a runoff election was required by the constitution. All save Hitler regarded it as purely a formality. The runoff was scheduled for April 10. With half a million storm troopers threatening to run riot in the interim, Hindenburg signed a decree holding them in check. Röhm, always pugnacious, would have taken this as a signal for insurrection; but Hitler, mindful of the Munich putsch, adhered to his pledge of staying within the law and so bowed to the decree. Campaigning was further damped down by a government pronouncement calling for a truce until April 3, allegedly to maintain tranquillity throughout Easter week. Thus, the active campaign was foreshortened to little more than a week. Hitler did what he could. He flew all over Germany, the picture of political vitality. Hindenburg roused himself not once to speak and false rumors spread that he was on his deathbed. Still, the electorate seemed to prefer a moribund Hindenburg to a raving Hitler, and he received the necessary majority of 53 percent. A miss seemed as good as a mile and a substantial gain in Nazi votes was small consolation to Hitler.

The election for president was lost and never to be contested again, but there remained an unhealthy Reichstag and its faltering chancellor, Brüning, whose decrees of lower wages and restrictions on finance and business had earned him the nickname, the Hunger Chancellor. Very soon after the presidential elections he took a fatal step by outlawing the SS and the SA. This was taken by the conservative right as an invitation to the communist workers to run wild. As champion for the conservative cause, General von Schleicher, (whose name meant "sly intriguer") entered the lists in their behalf. He characterized the Nazis as little children who needed to be guided by the hand, and with this error in mind he approached Hitler secretly in May. If Hitler would not attack a new government of the right, Schleicher would lift the ban on his black and brown armies. Hitler promised, and Schleicher proceeded to maneuver Brüning out of office. Franz von Papen, a former staff officer and member of the Prussian nobility, took his place. With Schleicher managing Papen, and Papen with the army behind him manipulating Hitler, the intended result was a strong nationalistic Germany. So Schleicher imagined, but if he conceived of himself as a master of political manipulation, he was unwittingly up against a Machiavellian master.

No sooner had Franz von Papen been named chancellor by Hindenburg on June 1, 1932, than he dissolved the unmanageable Reichstag once again. On the fifteenth the ban on the storm troopers was lifted, with Reichstag elections set for the last day of July. Ignoring his pledges to Schleicher, Hitler again took to the air with a whirlwind campaign, making appearances in fifty cities during the final two weeks, drawing devoted crowds everywhere. One mob waited under drenching skies for six hours while Hitler's plane buzzed about in the murky skies looking for a place to land.

Four distinct power blocks contested this election. First, there was Papen's right-wing conservatives, upper class industrialists and land owners for the most part, supported by the army and the eighty-five-year-old Hindenburg in whose hands the real power to govern was concentrated. Though powerful, this group represented no more than one-tenth of the voting public. Then there was the battered Weimar bunch, a conglomerate of middle class, middle-of-the-road parties, headed by the Social Democrats and still clinging to the much maligned idea of a German republic. Though battered, they still attracted wide public support. Finally, there were the two totalitarian extremes, the communist revolutionaries on the left, the Nazi reactionaries on the right.

A Vienna paper on election eve came out with the blaring

headlines: "HEIL SCHICKLGRUBER." The revelation of Hitler's less than distinguished ancestry did little to stem the National Socialist tide. Nearly fourteen million votes, or 37.3 percent of the total, went to the Nazis, more than the sum amassed by his closest rivals. In the Reichstag 230 seats were taken over by the Nazis from a total of 608. Social Democrats vacated all but 133 seats. The communists claimed 89. It was a victory for the Nazis but not a commanding one. The Reichstag remained divided as ever and on September 12, Göring, as the newly elected president of the Reichstag, helped to initiate yet another round of elections by leading the members in a resounding vote of no-confidence in Chancellor von Papen, 512 to 42.

Perhaps Hitler and supporters were worn out by too much campaigning. Perhaps the German people were benumbed by all the shouting. In any event, the new campaign got off to a poor start. In August, Hitler's neglected mistress, Eva Braun, had attempted suicide. This might have been a distraction. Far more detrimental was Goebbels's conduct in Berlin. The Reds had begun a wildcat strike of Berlin transport workers, demanding a pay increase; Goebbels directed his party members to join the picket lines. Storm troopers and communists together tore up streetcar tracks and stoned would-be strikebreakers. Though Hitler protested the impropriety of his Berlin disciples, the damage was done. Many middle-class supporters were alienated and the flow of campaign funds from businessmen became a trickle.

Sunday, November 6, told the story. The Nazis lost thirty-four seats in the Reichstag and two million popular votes. Their irresistible march to triumph seemed finally in retreat, and though they remained a strong party, the Nazi myth had palled. Failure brought Hitler to a realization. He would never overturn the system by Reichstag election. The other route to power was by way of political intrigue in high places. With the machinery of parliament still grinding its gears, effective power lay with the president and the close circle about him. Not by votes but by influencing a heretofore contemptuous Hindenburg could Hitler hope to succeed to the chancellorship.

Hitler might never have made the jump on his own but he had an unwitting ally in General von Schleicher. Ever intriguing, Schleicher set about undermining his protégé, Papen, who on his own could only create national chaos if he were to try again to form a government. Though Hindenburg had developed a personal fondness for the floundering Papen, he accepted the road of least resistance by requesting Schleicher to form a new government. As though it was not what he had all along desired, Schleicher protested, "I am the last horse in your stable and ought to be kept in reserve." This objection proved little more than a gesture. On December 2, 1932, Kurt von Schleicher became the first general-chancellor since Bismarck's replacement in 1890.

Schleicher, after all his manipulations, was not to last long. He took office convinced that with support from Hindenburg and the army he could "domesticate" Hitler. In fact, he would last less than two months. One of his first acts as chancellor was secretly to seek the aid of Gregor Strasser. If Strasser could have been detached from Hitler as Schleicher's vice-chancellor, the Nazi party would have been split and probably neutralized, but the supposedly secret talks came to Hitler's attention thanks to Papen, who took great pleasure in thus paying back Schleicher for his own dismissal. Hitler accused Strasser of treason. Strasser might have done better to embrace this idea and make the most of it. "Herr Hitler, I am no more traitor than any other willing messenger," he protested, then resigned from the party, picked up his family in Munich, and went on vacation in Italy, leaving Hitler to repudiate his name and his followers.

1933

Nineteen thirty-three was the year of reckoning; throughout January events moved rapidly. While Schleicher still groped for support in the parliament, his embittered protégé Papen continued to erode his shaky foundations. On the eighteenth he met privately with Hitler at the apartment of Joachim von Ribbentrop, a liquor salesman. Hitler demanded the chancellorship. Papen hedged, saying he lacked such influence, but went the following day to sound out the president. Hindenburg remained opposed to the idea, though his options were narrowing. Three days passed. Then Schleicher made a final desperate gamble. He admitted that he had failed to split the Nazi party or assemble a parliamentary basis for his cabinet. The alternative, he suggested, was for Hindenburg to dissolve the Reichstag, declare a state of emergency, and under Article 48 of the constitution, grant the chancellor powers to rule by decree. The result amounted to military dictatorship, a last chance to thwart Hitler, but Hindenburg was weary of Schleicher's endless plottings. He told the chancellor to keep trying for Reichstag support.

Unfortunately, word of Schleicher's proposals became public knowledge. The center parties, along with the Social Democrats, called Schleicher an enemy of the people, and when he weakly insisted that he had no intention of violating the constitution, his rightist support which would have condoned military rule also lost faith in him. Schleicher, the schemer, was backed into a corner and he finally knew it. On January 28 he resigned.

The president, who as much as anyone had created the vacancy, wanted his former favorite Papen back in harness. But Papen had failed once and besides, Schleicher suggested to the old general, they might easily use Hitler for their own purposes. Never had foolishness and senility so combined in a disastrous decision. Senility, at least, seems to have had misgivings, as Hindenburg was heard to lament, "Is it then my unsavory task to name this fellow Hitler as chancellor?" No voice was raised in opposition.

HITLER SUPREME

On January 30, 1933, Hitler was invited to form a government. That night jubilant Nazis tramped the streets of Berlin in endless torchlight parades. Hitler of course was ecstatic. Fate had again moved him along the path so long set out. Meanwhile, the ingenuous Papen bragged to his friends, "We have hired him for our business. Within two months we will push Hitler so tightly into the corner that he'll squeak." Indeed Papen was delighted, having finished off Schleicher and having tamed the Nazi wildman with a single stroke. With anyone else but Hitler this expectation might not seem so far from the mark. After all, in Hitler's eleven-man cabinet only three were Nazis. The other eight were conservatives in basic ideological agreement. Surely, it was reasonable to assume that Hitler's willingness to accept this situation attested to his intention to cooperate. Of course, Hitler was not reasonable, but there were few who realized this at the time. Papen's miscalculations embraced not only the conservative members of the cabinet but the majority of Social Democrats in the Reichstag, who were confident that it was impossible for Hitler to gain a two-thirds majority required to alter the Weimar Constitution. Businessmen and generals both supposed that if they gave support to Hitler he would, as any other politician, repay them a debt of service once he assumed office.

To the end, the forces of potential opposition outnumbered those loyal to Hitler. But they either naïvely trusted in the strength of democratic institutions and the force of reasonable argument or wasted their strength in mutual opposition, blindly ignoring the real enemy in their midst.

From this point onward, Hitler was beyond persuasion. There had been Dietrich Eckart and others in the early formative days who influenced his thinking, but now he could shout at Otto Strasser, "I never make a mistake. Every one of my words is historic." And to historic ends, the renewal of Aryan blood, *Lebensraum,* and the elimination of Jews, that dark, unlistening, and unswerving soul would now be dedicated. Iron-willed, coldly ruthless, power-obsessed, the Third Reich would never have been born on January 30, 1933, without this single man. "The thousand-year Reich" was his boast, but the life of the Nazi state would span only twelve years and three months, brief in terms of history but long enough for the most savage upheaval the world had ever known.

ACT III: GERMANY TODAY, 1933-39

THE REICHSTAG FIRE

The chancellorship was by no means Hitler's final goal. He intended to become dictator over a nazified Germany and he wanted to do it quickly for, remembering his mother's death, he now had a terror that cancer was creeping upon him. "I do not have the time to wait" prompted more than one drastic decision.

This first period of takeover, called innocently enough *Gleichschaltung* ("coordination"), began with preparations for new Reichstag elections. Hitler wanted a chance to overcome the November reversals, and with the machinery of government in his hands, he saw every prospect for a smashing victory. Elections were set for March 5, 1933.

A much debated event intervened. On February 28, 1933, the Reichstag building was gutted by flames. Whether it was the deed of a solitary Dutch communist, who was tried and executed, or a subtle plot abetted by the Nazis themselves has never entirely been resolved, and is really incidental to the use Hitler made of the fire. Goebbels seems to have been the first to appreciate its propaganda value. "Now I have them," he told Hitler; by "them" he was naming the communists. Göring, thinking along similar lines, put the police on emergency footing, and before the sun could rise on a smoldering Reichstag, four thousand people had been arrested, mostly communists, plus a few writers, doctors, and attorneys who had offended the Nazis.

Hitler was prompt to enlarge the import of the event, informing his vice-chancellor, Papen, "This is a signal from God. If, as I believe, this is communist work we must sweep out the murderous vermin with an iron fist." Though there was no evidence that a communist putsch was in the wind, Hitler insisted otherwise. At that morning's cabinet meeting he called for a "ruthless settling of accounts" with the Reds, who could expect no legal consideration. The next step was to request that Hindenburg sign an emergency decree.

THE EMERGENCY DECREE AND THE MARCH ELECTION

On February 28, Hindenburg signed a decree "for the Protection of the People and the State." In effect, this instrument suspended the constitution, allowing Hitler to arrest his opponents at will. No more important law was laid down during the Third Reich, for it provided the legal basis for all the otherwise illegal measures taken to solidify Nazism by way of persecution, terrorism, and repression.

Emboldened by the decree, truckloads of storm troopers rumbled through the streets beating up or lugging off opposition. Nazi terror reigned supreme until the day of the election, upon which Hitler expected the two-thirds majority needed to establish his dictatorship. Eighty-nine percent of the eligible voters braved the terrors of the street, and to Hitler's chagrin only 44 percent of those voted for National Socialism. True, along with the 52 seats won by their Nationalist party partners, they had a sufficient majority to conduct the daily Reichstag business for the first time in many years, but they had no absolute mandate. The Social Democrats still held 120 seats, the communists 81.

THE ENABLING ACT

Thwarted by the German public, Hitler kept battering at the doors to power. On March 23 the Reichstag convened at the Kroll Opera House while SS detachments patrolled outside, as much to intimidate the delegates as to keep order.

The Enabling Act—its official title, the Law for the Removal of the Distress of People and Reich—was basically a summons for the Reichstag to commit suicide. Under its terms the power to make or change existing laws passed from them to the administration and this included the right to alter the constitution. Additionally the right to draft laws moved from the president to chancellor, in other words to Hitler exclusively. This momentous bill, putting an end to democratic practice, was approved by the Reichstag in a few minutes while outside Hitler's black-clad troopers shouted in resounding chorus, "We demand the Enabling Act or there'll be hell to pay." Only the Social Democrats stood firm with their "Nays," and the enabling act was passed, 441 in favor, 94 against. Thus, the Reichstag participated emphatically in exempting itself from further participation in German politics and Hitler had won virtually limitless freedom of action. So long as he continued to soothe the old president and the army, his street gangs would have their way.

Even the veneer of a democratic Reichstag was soon to vanish. On June 22 the Social Democratic party was outlawed as hostile to the nation and state. June 28 saw the end of the State and German National Front parties. The next day the German National party, allies in the original coalition with the Nazis, folded up, their offices having been raided the week before by storm troopers. July 1 brought an end to the Center Association; the third of July tolled for the Young German Order. On the fourth, both the Bavarian People's party and the German People's party vanished. Finally, on the fifth, the Center party collapsed and within nine days a new law decreed: "The National Socialist German Workers' party constitutes the only political party in Germany."

COMMUNISTS—JEWS—LABOR

In the past storm troopers and communists had contested the streets on fairly equal terms. Now, three days after the formation of Hitler's cabinet, communist meetings were banned in Prussia. To enforce such measures, there was a new and ominous agency. A minor department in the Berlin police, detailed to watch anticonstitutional activities, was put under Göring's command. As of April 26, 1933, this old Department IA of the Prussian political police was replaced by the Geheime Staatspolizei ("Secret State Police"), better known as the Gestapo. Within two years its actions would be free from judicial review and it would take its place beside the SD (Sicherheitsdienst, or "Security Service") and the security branch of the SS in a sadistic competition to achieve the totalitarian state.

All these special police establishments, together with the more overt efforts of the storm troopers, made it impossible for a communist party to function openly and the party disappeared. An atmosphere of terrorism prevailed. There were illegal predawn arrests, torture, and incarceration. The SA delighted in such measures as forcing their prisoners to spit on Lenin's picture, gag down castor oil, chew up and swallow old dirty socks, but more important to the repression of communism was the removal of a right to a hearing, which meant in most cases that a concentration camp was the final destination. About fifty of these were established by the SA in 1933. The following year after the Röhm purge they fell into the hands of the Totenkopfverbaende, the so-called SS "Death's Head units." The name derived from their skull and bones insignia which had come from the death or glory days of the Napoleonic wars when the cavalry of many nations wore such grim emblems. With the SS it would attain more sinister implications as humiliating prisons deteriorated into realms of torture and death.

Until this time Nazism was very much a function of communism—the other side of the revolutionary coin. Now, within Germany, National Socialism stood alone. Communism was gone as a counterweight.

The Jews, if their reviled relationship to Nazism had been simply that of expedient scapegoat, could now have been passed over. Hitler had arrived and did not need them in his further rise to dictator and conqueror. As unprincipled conqueror, he might well have enlisted their talents and loyalties, but Hitler had his principles and the Jews remained as ever the evil force behind all that sought to destroy the master race. As a myth they had to be crushed. As a reality within German borders they were a weak minority, so in practice the myth could be put aside and dealt with at Hitler's convenience.

Hindenburg himself had little patience with the new chancellor's anti-Semitism and wrote Hitler a letter objecting to the persecution of those Jews who had fought bravely for the fatherland in World War I. Indeed, while Hindenburg lived, Hitler was relatively restrained in his persecutions. Many foresighted Jews did leave the country. Others, accustomed to centuries of persecution, accepted this as just one more period of hard times which must be endured. After all, Jews in England and the United States were barred from the best clubs. A good many German Jews wishfully believed that Hitler's venom was reserved for the Eastern Jews who had begun flooding into Germany after World War I. A few Jews, thinking of themselves as Germans first and Jews second, requested the new minister of labor, Friedrich Syrup, to stop further immigration of Eastern Jews on the grounds that their presence stirred up anti-Semitism.

Not until 1936, with Hindenburg dead and Hitler in sole command, was persecution seriously escalated. On September 13, during the Nuremburg party rally, Hitler raised the specter of the almost forgotten party protocol by announcing the Law for the Protection of German Blood and Honor. Henceforth, only those of "German or related blood" could be citizens. This event marked a deterioration of the Jewish lot in Nazi Germany, but the monstrous "final solution," instrumented under the *Lebensraum* program, remained unimaginable in 1935.

Communists and Jews might have expected little better on the basis of Hitler's past performance. Labor, though a portion of its membership merged with the communist left, seemed to be in for gentler treatment. They had, in theory, been part of the National Socialist program from the beginning. Reassuringly, Hitler declared May 1, 1933, a Day of National Labor. Labor was flattered. A big rally was held that night at the Tempelhof airport. There, Hitler warmed a crowd of several hundred thousand with his praise of labor's dignity and the need for unification behind the nation. His listeners cheered themselves hoarse. Patriotic songs were sung. Rockets flowered in the sky.

Bright and early the next day regular police, together with detachments of SS and SA, occupied union headquarters throughout the land. Leading officials were arrested and dispatched to concentration camps. The Labor Federation's banks and businesses were seized. Files were confiscated. Labor newspapers were shut down. Within three weeks the right to strike and to bargain collectively were removed, with decision-making left entirely to the "natural leaders," the employers, a far cry from the socialistic goals espoused by so many early Nazis.

Hitler, meanwhile, informed the disgruntled workers that they would be better off as part of the New German Labor Front. In reaction, there was not even an organized protest, let alone an uprising which the communist leadership would undoubtedly have encouraged had it not already been removed. From marching to the old "International" (the communist anthem), the workers now marched to a Nazi tune without ever breaking stride. For the duration of the Third Reich the workers were industrial serfs, secure enough in their jobs but with a share in the national income that was even below the Depression level. As the economy moved toward war, a special decree on June 22, 1938, instituted the conscription of labor. This commanded each German to work where the state assigned him, with the reciprocal assurance that he would not be fired without government approval.

Besides this guarantee of security, the state brought one more rigid benefit to the worker. For his cheap amusement there was the state-run Kraft Durch Freude ("Strength through Joy") program, which organized all his leisure and ·vacation time into sporting and travel groups. Individuality, as far as the Nazi state was concerned, no longer existed.

THE RÖHM PURGE

"Before foreign enemies are vanquished, the enemy within must be annihilated," Hitler had said. With the communist left in complete rout, only two independent power centers remained in Germany: the army and the storm troopers, and these two were incompatible. One must be chosen as friend, the other as foe.

The SA, ever expanding, eager for revolutionary action, were urged on by their leader Ernst Röhm, who liked to observe, "The brown tide [SA] must drown the gray rock [the army]." Hitler wanted no such clash. He remembered the Munich putsch and had vowed never to move into open conflict with the army again. Then, too, the SA militia with their small arms was a defensive force at best. Only the army possessed the heavy weapons needed for the world conquests ahead. Hitler's hope was to alleviate the nearing confrontation by transforming the SA into an unarmed propagandist force, obediently serving his political aims. The army, on the other hand, was to be built up into his instrument of attack, and Hitler's decision early in 1934 to restore compulsory military service within the regular army format was a slap at Röhm's desire to enlarge the SA into a nationwide militia which would eventually absorb the army into its ranks.

To this end, Röhm began calling for a "second revolution." With nearly three million men under his command, Röhm's words could not be taken lightly: "Anyone who thinks the task of the SA has been accomplished must become accustomed to the idea that we are here and intend to stay. . . . Whether they like it or not, we shall continue our struggle. Along with them, if they at last grasp what is at stake. Without them, if they don't wish to grasp it. And against them, if so it must be."

Such statements infuriated the generals of the army, and with Hindenburg clearly failing in the spring of 1934, Hitler had to think ahead. He would need their support when Hindenburg died, first in order to assume the vacated office of president, and second to forestall a restoration of the Hohenzollern monarchy which Hindenburg and many of the officers favored. To prepare the way for this support, Hitler proposed to the generals that if they backed his succession to the presidency, he, in return, would reduce the size of the SA and designate the army and navy as the only arms-bearers in the Third Reich. This pledge was made on May 16, 1934, and at that time Hitler had not decided how he would make it good.

He was, of course, open to suggestions. Göring, Goebbels, and Himmler, all at this time rivals for Röhm's power, began to conspire, spinning the false fabric of an impending SA putsch to unseat Hitler and carry through the "second revolution" along the more socialistic lines Röhm had always espoused. This concocted plot had no basis in fact. If nothing else, Röhm was an open and direct soldier. If he refused to kowtow to Hitler's more conservative ideas, he trusted Hitler as a friend and refused to believe Hitler would fall in with a plot against the SA. So when the time came for the SA summer holidays, Röhm relaxed at the Hanslbauer Hotel at Wiessee with the overthrow of his beloved führer the furthest thing from his mind.

Meanwhile, Goebbels, Göring, and Himmler were converting Hitler, no difficult job as he needed a case against the SA to placate the army, and even for Hitler it was always easier to kill loyal friends once they had been transformed into villains. "I gave the order to shoot those who were the ringleaders in this treason, and I further gave the order to burn down to the raw flesh the ulcers of this poisoning of the wells of our domestic life," he proclaimed later in words again reminiscent of his mother's cancer and the cancer he always feared was latent in himself.

In the early hours of June 30, 1934, Hitler set the purge in motion. While Göring and Himmler were rounding up 150 SA leaders in Berlin to be summarily shot at the Lichterfelde Cadet School, Hitler led a column of cars to the hotel where the vacationing Röhm slumbered. As there was no SA plot afoot, most of the victims died in complete confusion. There were no trials, no evidence, no verdicts. They were simply slaughtered.

At first Hitler could not bring himself to condemn Röhm to death. The bewildered Röhm waited until July 1 in a Munich prison and then, with Hitler's mind finally resolved, he was given a pistol loaded with one bullet and told to do the honorable thing. Refusing to take part in such a mockery, he said, "If I am to be killed let Adolf do it himself." But Hitler had no stomach for personally taking life and two SS officers did the job with pistols at point-blank range.

Though the purge was designed to bring the SA into line, it was an occasion to settle other accounts, some new, some old. Two Gestapo agents appeared in General von Schleicher's study. Given time enough only to say *"Ja,"* the former chancellor who had conspired to block Hitler's political path was riddled with bullets. His frantic wife was also cut down as she rushed to his side. Gregor Strasser, long a thorn in Hitler's side, was apprehended while taking lunch, removed to the Prinz Albrechtstrasse Gestapo prison. An unidentified gunman began shooting at him through the cell bars. Like a caged animal, Strasser dodged away at first but was finally brought down. Someone entered the cell to deliver the coup de grâce. Going back further, there was old state commissioner Gustav von Kahr who had thwarted Hitler's Beer Hall Putsch in 1923. His body turned up in a swamp near the Dachau concentration camp. It had been hacked with pickaxes.

The means were brutal and bloody. Hitler is said to have suffered from nervous indigestion for days; but without becoming indebted to anyone, he had put an end to the SA's revolutionary ideas, satisfied the army, forestalled any return of the Hohenzollerns, and appeased public complaints about SA street violence. The puppet Reichstag immediately and unanimously passed a bill legalizing the murders as "emergency defense measures of the state," thus ending any illusions that Hitler and his supporters would be legally or morally restrained in the future. Up until now, an argument might have been made that violence was unavoidable in revolutionary times, but henceforth the belief in the rule of law and order could not survive such lawless slaughter.

The army, gullible as all the rest, saw the elimination of "the brown trash," as they called the SA, as their victory. By Hitler's repudiating the SA, he was clearly disarming himself and placing the Nazi party at the mercy of the generals. They took little note that on July 20, 1934, Hitler freed the SS from its subordination to the SA, making it an independent organization directly under his authority; in time the SS would become a state and army unto itself, realizing most of Röhm's ambitions.

The democratic constitution and parliamentary government were gone. The political parties that had blocked Hitler's way were disbanded. Communism had been driven from the streets, the workers chained to their assembly lines, and the storm troopers retired into permanent subservience. "We have the power today. Nobody can offer us any resistance. But now we must educate German man for this new State," Hitler said. In other words, all those national institutions which make up a modern state had to be nazified. As these groups were not in open opposition, violence was not in order, but no less strict subordination was in the offing.

HINDENBURG DIES

Hitler's rise to power had been meteoric, but two sources of potential resistance remained: the army and the eighty-seven-year-old Hindenburg. In the summer of 1934 the latter was clearly dying, and on August 2, as he breathed his last, Hitler's cabinet contrived a law merging the role of chancellor and president. Though Hindenburg expired with the words, "My kaiser. My fatherland," it was now the führer to whom all allegiance was to be pledged. As such, Hitler ranked as the supreme commander of the armed forces, and wasting no time, he called his chief of staff, General Werner von Blomberg, and the commanders of the army, navy, and air force and obliged them to repeat the following oath: "I swear before God to give my unconditional obedience to Adolf Hitler, Führer of the Reich and its people, Supreme Commander of the Armed Forces, and I pledge my word as a brave soldier to observe this oath always even at the risk of my life."

The military thus pledged its soul to the devil, and on August 19 the German voters did likewise in a plebiscite, 90 percent freely giving their approval of Adolf Hitler as Hindenburg's successor. Could he demand more? For a time it seemed not. Germany quieted down. Even Jewish emigration diminished. It was only a pause for Hitler to draw a deep breath.

THE ARMY

General von Blomberg on July 3, 1934, had congratulated the chancellor on purging the storm troopers, a first step toward making common cause with lawlessness. A month later he gave his oath of loyalty to the Führer, but even so Hitler was not content. During the Munich putsch, generals had made promises of faith and betrayed them. And as an Austrian, Hitler retained a basic contempt for these strutting Prussians as they, aristocrats of the old school, could not shake off the thought that their führer was no gentleman but an ill-bred bohemian corporal.

He would be rid of them and he would begin at the top. Like so many of Hitler's victims General von Blomberg furnished the ingredients of his own downfall. A widower, he married his secretary, Erna Gruhn, on January 12, 1938. Hitler appeared as a witness. With the happy couple away on honeymoon, it became public knowledge that the former Miss Gruhn had been a prostitute. Hitler, particularly as he had been part of the wedding, was furious. Even the army cooperated in demanding Blomberg's resignation, and dismissal followed on January 25. It might be added that the marriage remained a happy one and outlived the Third Reich.

Blomberg's obvious successor was General Werner von Fritsch, but Hitler saw the chance to remove another troublesome Prussian. On the same day as Blomberg's dismissal a trumped-up charge was brought against Fritsch. He was accused of having committed criminal homosexual acts with two Hitler Youths, not to mention a male prostitute by the name of Bavarian Joe. The outraged and innocent Fritsch demanded a trial. Realizing this would have turned out badly for the prosecution, Hitler sidestepped the confrontation and ordered Fritsch on indefinite leave.

When Blomberg could suggest no successor to his position, Hitler inquired who was the head of his staff. It was the uninspired General Wilhelm Keitel whom Blomberg described as "nothing but the man who runs my office." Hitler was delighted; Keitel was just the sycophantic errand-runner he had in mind, for he wished no rivalry from the supreme military command.

Just before midnight on February 4, 1938, Hitler's decree was made public. Sixteen generals were dismissed, along with Fritsch and Blomberg. Forty-four others were transferred. Without encountering a grumble of opposition, Hitler had eliminated the last potential source of serious opposition in Germany. Curiously, Hitler, who has been called the ultimate militarist, was quite the opposite. His dictatorship was basically civilian and completely dominated the armed forces. In World War I the generals had run the country. From now on they were merely instruments of an ex-corporal's ambitions, with traditional German militarism so altered that it could not survive the Third Reich.

JUSTICE IN HITLER'S GERMANY

The law courts have been called the last refuge for individual rights. At first the German courts seemed to hold their own against Hitler, most notably in the Reichgericht ("Supreme Court"), which tried the Dutch communist Marinus Van der Lubbe and three others for burning the Reichstag. The trial took place in the autumn of 1933, before Hitler's grip had really tightened. Only Van der Lubbe was condemned, despite threats upon the jurists from Göring: "You wait until we get you outside this court," and "You would think we were on trial, not the communists." Hitler remained calm, remarking, *"Mein lieber* Göring, it is only a question of time."

As usual, he made good on his words. The Reichsgericht henceforth was shorn of jurisdiction over treason and a new court was created for that purpose, the Volksgerichtshof ("People's Court"). This was to become a dreaded instrument of Nazi terror. Even most of the defense lawyers were devoted Nazis, and when the widow of Dr. Erich Klausener, a Catholic Action leader eliminated in the Röhm purge, brought an action for damages against the state, it was quashed by having her attorneys lodged in Sachsenhausen concentration camp until the suit was withdrawn.

Hitler, in other words, was the law, and this was emphasized on April 7, 1933, by the Civil Service Law which required the dismissal of all judges who were not "politically reliable." Any person who slipped through this net of Nazi justice was far from safe. As likely as not, upon stepping into the street, an acquitted individual would be picked up by the Gestapo, whose actions were not reviewable by any court.

BIG BUSINESS AND THE UPPER CLASS

Communism imagined a stateless utopia after eliminating upper-class capitalism. Nazism aspired to the all-powerful state, and was quite willing to make use of its tycoons. Hitler wanted no bloody revolution. He had no intention of murdering the golden goose as had been done in Russia, and the old Prussian nobility delighted in the evident renewal of military spirit. Many joined the army as well as the SS, whose officers' corps became well stocked with Prussians.

The new, at first camouflaged, war economy promised big government contracts to businessmen. But it was not all cakes and ale for the capitalists. They had applauded when Hitler had chained labor to the production lines. Now they found themselves being manacled as well. True, profits were up, but the Reich Economic Chamber told them what to make, how much to make, and at what price to sell. Taxes were high and getting higher. In October 1937 came the real crackdown. In the interest of national efficiency all corporations having capital less than $40,000 were dissolved. No new ones could be formed unless they represented a $2-million investment or more. The result was the termination of many small businesses, while larger ones combined into cartels. Large or small, all took their directives from the state.

THE CHURCHES

As the repository for Christian virtues, the churches fared little better than other institutions under Nazism. Hitler had been raised as a devout Catholic and he always considered himself religious, but insofar as the churches opposed him, he hated them as man-made institutions.

Little opposition might be expected from the domestic Protestant Church, whose founder, Martin Luther, had been a passionate anti-Semite and believer in state power. For the most part, it bowed to Nazi dominion under the slogan, "One People, One Reich, One Faith." There were exceptions. Notable among them was a former submarine commander from World War I, the Reverend Martin Niemöller who at first welcomed, then rejected, Nazism. His opposition led to arrest in 1937 and brief imprisonment. Release in 1938 brought not freedom but the Gestapo's "protective custody," which lasted until Nazism collapsed in 1945. Hundreds of other leading pastors were arrested. Many died in prison, but apart from leaving a legacy of courage and dignity, their efforts were to no avail. The majority, of course, did not hazard imprisonment for freedom of worship, and were won over by Hitler's successes and Germany's growing prestige.

Though international in scope, the Catholic Church achieved no greater measure of independence. As early as 1923 a Catholic theologian at Munich University was proclaiming, "Away with the specter of worldwide pacifism. Away with the disgrace of the League of Nations. What we need is a great Siegfried but he must not delay too long." German Catholics of this bent, and there were many, fearing atheistic communism and longing for German revival, were all too eager to embrace Nazism. For those who protested, there were concentration camps, and many priests and nuns joined their Protestant brothers there. As early as 1933 the Catholic Youth League, a rival of the Hitler Youth, was dissolved by the state and Catholic publications were suppressed. For a true Christian to speak out in Nazi Germany was to court summary martyrdom, a role more admired than emulated, and these principled few were quickly hauled from the pulpit.

THE FARMERS

The Great Depression had left the German farmer in a bad way. In 1933 Hitler set up the Reich Food Estate to supervise production, marketing, and processing. Under a Blut und Boden ("Blood and Soil") program, the farmer was told how he was the salt of the earth and the bedrock of the Third Reich. In practical terms he was treated like other special interest groups; that is, prices for his products rose but otherwise his existence was circumscribed by higher costs, and limitations on what and how much he could market. The almost medieval Hereditary Farm Law of September 29, 1933, characterized his secure but limited existence. Under its terms, all farms up to 308 acres (125 hectares) that could provide a family a decent living became hereditary estates. This meant they could not leave the family by sale or mortgage, but had to pass by inheritance to the nearest heir. Behind this program was the remembrance of World War I and the Allied blockade which nearly starved Germany to death. With another war in mind, Hitler longed for German self-sufficiency and a stable, controlled farm population was a major step in that direction.

THE ARTS AND MASS MEDIA

Radio, press, film, theater, even music and the fine arts came under the dominion of Goebbel's Propaganda Ministry. All must serve the purposes of Nazism or suffer the consequences. By spring of 1933 the *Gleichschaltung* of radio broadcasting was complete. Broadcasters and their material had been nazified. More cumbersome was the problem of controlling Germany's three-thousand-odd newspapers. Economic pressure eliminated many of the smaller ones. Others had to be confiscated, while the Reich Press Law of October 4, 1933, made journalism a public vocation and required all editors to be of the Aryan race and German citizenship. In the end only papers that adhered to the Nazi party line survived.

Similar criteria were applied to theater, literature, and films. Even painting—due to Hitler's obsession that modern art was senseless and depraved—was publicly restricted. Music fared a bit better, as it was the furthest removed from the political world, but the works of Jewish composers could not be played and Jewish musicians were rooted out of the orchestras. Like modern art, modern music such as jazz which had originated with "degenerate" American blacks was curtailed. Germans had to think and see and hear only in Aryan terms and those who did otherwise were in trouble.

EDUCATION: PROFESSORS AND STUDENTS

Since Bismarck's day, German professors had strayed from their humanitarian traditions to the realm of chauvinistic politics. Heinrich von Treitschke and others have already been discussed and this tendency existed into the twentieth century. Crushed by the defeat of 1918, many were ready to embrace the stab-in-the-back myth without ever helping their students to understand the realities of the situation. Even more than the university professors, the younger secondary school teachers, many of whom were disillusioned veterans, used their classrooms as sounding boards for their frustrated dreams of German glory. Many textbooks were nationalistic and antidemocratic, with stress upon the majestic German past.

This left the teaching profession as a whole receptive to Hitler's ascension to power. As the so-called *Wegbereiters* ("path finders") German educators were all too eager to disseminate National Socialism. Very little pressure was required to get them into step, while those who spoke in opposition or had Jewish blood vanished from the ranks. So great was their National Socialist zeal that many began teaching "German" math, physics, and chemistry, giving to formerly pure sciences an absurd racial slant. The result was a decline in academic standards and scientific achievement, which in part can be thanked for such blessings as Germany's inability to create an atomic bomb during the war.

With such susceptibility on the part of their teachers, it is hardly surprising that their student bodies were among the vanguard of the National Socialist movement. As of 1930, 60 percent of German students derived from the lower-middle class, who comprised the hard core of National Socialism. More than 30 percent came from the upper-middle class, who, if not immediately converted, were naturally nationalistic.

Once Nazism took over the government, few students resisted its all-pervasive assault. Kindergarden children in Cologne had to recite the following before lunch each day:

Führer, my Führer, bequeathed to me by God.
Protect and preserve me as long as I live!
You have rescued Germany from deep despair.
I thank you for my daily bread.
Abide long with me. Forsake me not.
Führer, my Führer, my faith and my light.
    Heil, my Führer!

School graduates were obliged to register with the Labor Exchange because "the foremost goal is not the enrichment of individual existence but the increasing prosperity of the nation." There was no escaping Nazi indoctrination.

In this spirit, students and professors alike took part in the event most symbolic of Germany's abdication of the will to think. On May 10, 1933, with SA and SS bands booming out patriotic tunes, a torchlight procession wound down Berlin's Unter den Linden to make a funeral pyre of "un-German" books. Up in flames went much of the world's great literature. As Goebbels explained it: "The spirit of the German people can again express itself. These flames not only illuminate the final end of an old era, they also light up the new." But a hundred years before, the poet Heinrich Heine had spoken with greater wisdom: "Where books are burned, in the end men will burn as well."

THE HITLER YOUTH

Nazism was not content to leave indoctrination of the young to the school system. Here were the pliable minds and supple bodies that would carry the Third Reich into the future, and it was Hitler's goal as early as the 1920s to bring young people from all walks of life together and indoctrinate them with National Socialist policies and propaganda. No other group was so malleable, and by the end of 1932 the Hitler Youth organization had over 100,000 members. It would eventually grow to some eight million, the largest youth organization in the world. In Hitler's words: "We must develop organizations in which an individual's entire life can take place. Then every activity and every need of every individual will be regulated by the collectivity represented by the party." Robert Ley, minister of the Labor Front, expressed it more simply: "We begin with the child when he is three years old. As soon as he begins to think he gets a little flag put in his hands."

When plans for organizing children below the age of ten into the Hitler Youth were put forward, a popular joke went around calling them the AA men, a pun on SA. In German baby talk, AA was a synonym for excrement, and so these were the storm troopers still in diapers. In fact, from age six to eighteen the Hitler Youth program was a deadly serious business. Six-year-olds were ushered in as Pimpfs ("Little Ones"), graduated at ten into the Jungvolk ("Young Folk"), when this oath was taken: "In the presence of this blood banner, which represents our Führer, I swear to devote all my energies and my strength to the savior of our country, Adolf Hitler." In the Jungvolk a boy would learn to read semaphores, lay telephone wires, perform small-arms drills with air guns and dummy hand grenades, repair bicycles, and, of course, continue with Nazi indoctrination. The nucleus of the program were fourteen- to eighteen-year-olds. Upon graduation into the Hitler Youth proper, a boy was given a dagger on which was engraved "Blood and Honor," and pledged that from now on he must defend the brown shirt by force of arms. "We are born to die for Germany" was his ethos, and though many would do just that, the program itself was a vigorous affirmation of life; stressing group athletics, fighting for the team and never oneself, harvesting, charity work, and, of course, military and ideological preparations. Upon graduation, the eighteen-year-old served briefly in the Labor Service program and then moved on to the army.

So from age six most of a German boy's formerly free time was accounted for by Nazism. In 1938 the four million youths who had not entered the ranks voluntarily were conscripted as though into the army itself, with their parents informed that those who resisted would be taken from home and placed in orphanages.

Girls were not overlooked. At ten they joined the Jungmädel ("Young Maidens"), at fourteen the BDM, the Bund Deutscher Mädel ("League of German Maidens"), which featured sports, camping, singing party songs, memorizing a romanticized life of Hitler, and so forth. At eighteen they would have a year of farm service, after which presumably they would be given over to kitchen, church, and especially children: the mothering of another generation of Aryans with medals awarded to those who proved especially fruitful.

However sinister the purpose of the Hitler Youth, it was unquestionably effective in molding millions of healthy fanatical young Nazis. At the end of World War I, German courts were trying 100,000 cases of juvenile delinquency annually. By 1933 it was down to 16,000, a good indication of how well Hitler's Youth sublimated and redirected their criminal energies.

THE FÜHRER SUPREME IN GERMANY

Within a few years the whole structure of German society had been revamped, indoctrinated, turned to the purposes of one man. There is no denying Hitler's achievements. Unhampered by experience or morality, he shrank from no expediency to achieve his goals, however unlikely they might seem to more practical minds. Every German had lost liberty, while the state had gained prosperity and newfound pride in unity. Almost single-handedly, Hitler had ended unemployment, and vanquished the depression by insisting on rearmament, which in the end must lead to economic crisis. Few Germans thought this far ahead. After years of despair it was simply good to work, and all tasks were honorable; even, as Hitler said, "to sweep the streets as a citizen of this Reich" was a privilege. Unity of spirit and abounding self-confidence were his prime accomplishments, all the more remarkable as Hitler had no practical program to back them up. While communism called for the utopia of the working man, Hitler claimed to be the smasher of communism by harmonizing the goal of the working man with that of his capitalist boss, all for the enrichment of the state as a whole. Between the terror of communism in the east and the rot of capitalism in the west, his Germany rose a tower of strength.

It was a matter of single-minded passion that bound leader to people, theatrics without substance. Hitler left the day-to-day running of government to his subordinates, a chaos of competing underlings manipulating a sprawling and overlapping bureaucracy without notable efficiency. Hitler alone stood above the disorder as final arbiter, and where sound judgment failed, performance took over. During the great Party rallies at Nuremburg, which featured the unfurling of 20,000 flags and the convergence of 130 great searchlights upon Hitler, the Führer's voice echoed from countless loudspeakers. "We are strong and will get stronger," he pledged to his people, the bloodthirsty sheep as some would call them, a threat to the world. Thus, the popular will was rallied and the spectacular ceremonies constantly overlaid social and economic problems that would have stymied more practical planners.

Hitler had no time for plodding doubts. Since World War I, in the words of Eduard Spranger, "Everywhere in Germany there is a veritable expectation of a messiah." Hitler was that messiah, tied to a historical mission. "Ultimately," wrote Spranger, "the individual man is weak in all his nature and actions when he goes contrary to almighty providence and its will, but he becomes immeasurably strong the moment he acts in harmony with this Providence; then there pours down upon him that force which has distinguished all the great men of history." Hitler was fixated upon the goal of securing the Aryan race from the peril of a Judaic-communist menace. To this end he sought only power, not social reform, and his domestic policies were only adjuncts to this divinely inspired objective of lasting world dominion.

Hitler was far from alone in his sense of mission. Most Germans believed, carrying belief from the terrifying to the comically absurd, as exemplified by the lecturer who related an experience with a talking dog which responded to the question "Who is Adolf Hitler?" with the clear words *"Mein Führer."* If dogs could believe it, how could Hitler think otherwise? No longer did he read voraciously. No longer did he respond to opinions of others. Clearly he was infallible, and he lived from now on in deepening mental isolation. So vast did he see himself that all other leaders and the nations they represented diminished. Increasingly, he would underrate his opponents—England, the USSR, and finally the United States of America—and this would lead to his ultimate destruction. But in Germany of the mid-1930s he could do no wrong. He had successfully unleashed the pent-up dynamism of a warlike people and that, as he said, was "the final goal of politics." Germany was his today; tomorrow he would try to seize the entire world.

ACT IV:
TOMORROW THE WORLD,
1933-41

HITLER THE PEACE LOVER

Even before National Socialism had achieved dominion over almost every aspect of German life, Hitler was considering his greater vision. No dreamer of a bucolic utopia, he could see only the front line extended on and on into conquered lands. This warrior instinct was supported by the most intensely nationalistic citizenry the world had ever known. Service to the fatherland was the highest ethical value, beside which considerations of political morality vanished.

This new Nazi nationalism was regarded with suspicion throughout Europe. It seemed to unite the great powers. Poland and France spoke of beginning a preventive war. But Germany was still weak. She could not yet afford to fight, so Hitler's first international task was that of peacemaker. On May 17, 1933, before the Reichstag he pledged to disarm if his neighbors did so; an easy offer, since Germany had very little disarming to do. And when his suggestion was disregarded, as he knew it would be, he withdrew Germany from the Disarmament Conference and the League of Nations on October 14. By mid-December he was planning on a conscript army of 300,000.

As continuing evidence of his peaceful intentions, Hitler concluded a surprise ten-year nonaggression pact with Poland on January 26, 1934. This treaty was a purely sham expediency on Hitler's part, but he did still entertain genuine hopes of persuading England to become an ally in his campaign against communism. Between them they would portion out the world; England to command the seas and her far-flung colonies, Germany to be supreme on the great Eurasian continent.

REARMING

With or without England, war was inevitable, and rearming a necessary prerequisite. On October 1, 1934, Hitler had informed his secret general staff, a body forbidden by the Versailles treaty, that the army must be built up with overt conscription to be announced in six months. The navy also was to be strengthened. Even during the Weimar Republic, forbidden submarine parts had been constructed in Finland, Holland, and Spain. While Versailles limited German warships to sixteen thousand tons per vessel, two twenty-six-thousand-ton battle cruisers were underway, disguised as "improved ten-thousand-ton ships." In these early days the air force, called civilian aviation, was also designing warplanes and training pilots in the League for Air Sports. Great Ruhr factories were working overtime, with the Krupp family turning out cannon, and I. J. Farben producing synthetic gasoline and rubber for self-sufficiency in the coming struggle. By the end of 1934, rearmament was on such a scale that the secret could not long be kept from the victors of World War I.

On Saturday, March 16, 1935 (Hitler regularly saved his surprises for weekends), he decreed universal military training and proposed an army of half a million men. The expected protests from France and England were turned aside with another peace speech: "The bloodshed on the European continent in the course of the last three hundred years bears no proportion to the national result of the events. In the end France has remained France, Germany, Germany. . . . The principal effect of every war is to destroy the flower of the nation . . . Germany needs peace and desires peace." It made such good sense, almost everyone believed him. On the very same day he quietly appointed Dr. Hjalmar Schacht plenipotentiary general over a war economy.

A naval treaty came next. Hitler was determined to enlarge Germany's naval strength to 35 percent of that enjoyed by England. The proposed agreement took the form of an ultimatum; English compliance on June 6, 1935, reaffirmed Hitler's belief that extortion could get him anything.

"A great hour in the history of our country has struck. . . . forty million Italians, a sworn community, will not let themselves be robbed of their place in the sun." These words were said by Mussolini as he stole the limelight on October 2, 1935, in justification of his imminent invasion of the small African country Ethiopia. This unexpected assault had one major drawback for Hitler. It tended to widen the gap between the two nations he envisioned as future world partners: England and Italy. In the end he would side with the militarily inept Italians. On the positive side, the Ethiopian war did distract world attention from Germany, and within the year, with Schacht as economic dictator, the Reich had embarked on a four-year plan of total war economy with the goal of complete self-sufficiency by 1940. Then let war come.

THE RHINELAND

Mussolini's little war also encouraged Hitler in his next step toward the brink. After World War I, a thirty-mile strip east of the Rhine River as well as all German territory on the west bank had been demilitarized as a precaution against that water barrier becoming a defensive west wall. On March 7, 1936, another Saturday, a token force of German soldiers occupied the Rhineland. Hitler was certain that England which, by simply closing the Suez Canal or declaring an oil embargo, might have derailed Italy's expeditionary force in Africa, would take no action against this lesser breach of the peace. The League of Nations made no move. France had the right and might to move in, with British support. It was a last chance for the allies of World War I to prevent a serious reenactment but they did nothing. England's Lord Lothian summed up the general attitude: "The Germans, after all, are only going into their own back garden." The German people almost to a man applauded their infallible Führer, and Hitler, after tirelessly pledging peaceful intentions, even proposed a nonaggression pact with France and Germany's return to the League of Nations, while at the same time beginning fortifications along this western frontier so that attention might be given to the east, and *Lebensraum.*

THE SPANISH INTERLUDE

On July 17, 1936, a military revolt began in Morocco and spread quickly into the Spanish civil war. Italy was quick to give massive assistance to the revolutionaries. Though of like sentiment, Hitler restricted his aid, since a prolonged Spanish struggle would hold the attention of England and France. Common interest was sufficient for him to enter a pact with Italy, which Mussolini would describe: "This Berlin-Rome line is not a diaphragm but rather an axis around which can revolve all those European states with a will to collaboration and peace." It was a decisive step indeed, for it ended any likelihood of Germany and England arriving at similar terms. English disapproval increased as Italian involvement in the Spanish civil war intensified, with a result that the "Axis" was becoming a permanent shackling of Germany and Italy, a bond that was to prove dead weight to Germany.

Meanwhile, Hitler was unveiling wider schemes. In a conference called on November 5, 1937, he stated that if he "still lived, it [is my] firm resolution to solve the question of German living space between 1943 and 1945 at the latest." Sooner if circumstances proved favorable.

AUSTRIA—THE *ANSCHLUSS*

In the past, Italy had considered itself Austria's protector. With the Axis pact in force, Hitler realized he would not be obstructed by Mussolini. England and France had time and again proved their cowardice. It was time for the German people of Austria to return to the greater Reich. The SA had long been active in Austria, and many Austrians aspired to the *Anschluss* ("union") of the two nations. The majority did not.

German pressure kept building up in the winter of 1937–38. The Austrian chancellor, Dr. Kurt von Schuschnigg, bravely stood his ground despite the Nazi murder of his predecessor, Engelbert Dollfuss. On February 11, 1938, he received an ultimatum from Hitler: "There is nothing to be discussed. I will not change one detail. You will either sign it as is and fulfill my demands within three days or I will order the march into Austria." Schuschnigg would not give up easily. As his support eroded, he turned to the Austrian people, proposing a plebiscite, asking if they wanted a "free, independent, social, Christian, and united Austria—yes or no." This vote was to be held on March 13.

If allowed, the plebiscite would have repudiated union with Germany. Hitler's hand was forced. He had to intervene, and he did so by putting pressure on old President Wilhelm Miklas to appoint Artur von Seyss-Inquart, a Nazi, as chancellor. Schuschnigg had run out of hope. No help was coming from England or Italy, and he resigned with the words, "Thus I take leave of the Austrian nation with a German farewell which also expresses my heartfelt wish: God save Austria!"

It remained only for Seyss-Inquart to invite Hitler to become Austria's new president. Then the German tanks moved in. "The populace saw that we came as friends and we were everywhere joyfully received," noted General Heinz Guderian. Hitler arrived in a caravan of cars, visiting his birthplace at Braunau am Inn near Vienna, and later Linz and the Danube bridge which he had hated as a boy. "That ugly thing still there. But not for long, you can be sure of that," he said.

The plebiscite which Schuschnigg had planned for March 13 was held on April 10, after an orgy of Nazi repression and sadism, during which storm troopers dragged Jews from their homes, forcing them to clean barracks toilets with their bare hands and to scrub old pro-Austrian slogans from walls and streets with acid. The result of the plebiscite was a foregone conclusion: a nearly unanimous vote to become part of greater Germany. So another bloodless victory had been achieved. Hitler's prestige soared.

MUNICH—PEACE IN OUR TIME

Hitler was insatiable. Every victory enlarged his appetite. As early as June 24, 1937, he had discussed with his generals a plan named "Case Green" concerned with a surprise attack on Czechoslovakia. With the absorption of Austria, many Germans residing in a part of Czechoslovakia called the Sudentenland began demonstrating under the slogan "Home to the Reich." Hitler had been digesting Austria for only two weeks when he met with the leader of these Sudeten Germans to discuss the problem. All Hitler needed was an excuse to invade, and three and a half million Sudeten Germans seemed eager to provide it by assuming the questionable role of mistreated minority.

Göring, rather than Hitler, sounded the first ominous blast: "A trivial bit of Europe is making life unbearable for mankind. The Czechs, a vile race of cultureless dwarfs—nobody even knows where they came from—are oppressing a civilized race; and behind them, together with Moscow, there can be seen the eternal face of the Jewish devil!"

Throughout the summer, Nazi propaganda inflated the crisis toward the point at which Hitler would feel justified in overrunning Czechoslovakia with his army. England and France, particularly England's prime minister Neville Chamberlain, entered the picture to mediate and what followed was the protracted Munich meetings. It was a time for the allies to stand firm. Together England and France remained militarily stronger than Germany, but when Hitler demanded a Sudeten plebiscite to determine whether the territory should attach itself to Germany, Chamberlain did not rebuke him. At all costs he wanted to avoid war and with Hitler smirking in the background Chamberlain urged the Czechs to submit to German demands until, on September 20, 1938, their president Eduard Beneš said: "We have relied upon the help that our friends might have given us, but when the question of reducing us by force arose, it became evident that the European crisis was taking on too serious a character. Our friends, therefore, advised us to buy freedom and peace by our sacrifice, and this in proportion to their own inability to help us. The president of the Republic and our government had no other choice, for we found ourselves alone."

Hitler had won, but he had not won enough. On September 21 he told the confused British prime minister, "I am terribly sorry, Mr. Chamberlain, but I can no longer discuss these matters; this solution (the plebiscite), after the occurrences of the last few days, is no longer practicable." What more could he want? Occupation of the Sudetenland by German troops was the answer. A horrified Chamberlain withdrew. Expecting refusal, Hitler began planning what he really wanted, military seizure of all Czechoslovakia; again an appeasing Chamberlain upset his designs. Chamberlain again put pressure on the Czechs, and on September 30 a pact was signed, with the German army to march into the Sudetenland, the occupation to be completed within ten days, all in the interest of "peace in our time," as Chamberlain phrased it.

Hitler thanked Chamberlain for his efforts toward peace and gave him the pledge that the Czech problem was the last territorial demand which he had to make in Europe. Even so, he was privately furious at having signed an agreement that fell short of taking over the entire country as he had done with Austria. Despite Chamberlain, there was talk in England of mobilizing the fleet and calling up the auxiliary air force. A bitter Winston Churchill spoke prophetically in the House of Commons: "All is over, silent, mournful, abandoned, broken Czechoslovakia recedes into the darkness." He further told the British people: "We have sustained a great defeat without a war, the consequences of which will travel far with us. . . . and do not suppose that this is the end. This is only the beginning of the reckoning."

In Germany there was the usual outburst of enthusiasm at another triumph without bloodshed. The army moved in to occupy the Sudetenland, followed closely by the Gestapo and Security Service whose job it was to root out "Marxist traitors and other enemies of the state."

CZECHOSLOVAKIA

Before Hitler could create artificial circumstances justifying the absorption of what remained of Czechoslovakia, an event occurred that represented a downward plateau in German morality. It was triggered on November 17, 1938, when a seventeen-year-old German-Jewish refugee assassinated the third secretary of the German embassy in Paris. That was all it took for the Nazis to organize, on the night of November 9, a "spontaneous pogrom of revenge against German Jews." Nearly a hundred were killed, some twenty thousand were arrested. Shops, homes and synagogues were burned. It would be remembered as Crystal Night for all the broken glass, and in the end, with heavy-footed irony, the Jews were obliged to pay for the destruction of their own property as the insurance funds otherwise due them were confiscated by the state.

Czechoslovakia had to wait until 1939. In his New Year's message Hitler wished for "German success in contributing to the German pacification of the world." That meant the Czechs. He needed only an excuse and in February Goebbels launched a vast propaganda campaign against the Czech government. For the first time Hitler was planning to conquer non-Germanic lands. "You know I am like a wanderer," he said to an aide, "who must cross an abyss on the razor's edge. But I must. I simply must cross." He set the fateful ides of March as the time to move. With the Sudetenland already in hand, Czechoslovakia had lost most of its defenses facing Germany. Either they submitted or they would be ruthlessly attacked. Having been abandoned by the great powers before, the president felt forced to call on the führer to bring domestic peace to Czechoslovakia. Hitler magnanimously agreed, guaranteeing them an autonomous development of their ethnic life as suited to their character.

Again, England and France were faced with an accomplished fact and did not budge. On March 15, right on schedule, German troops moved into Czechoslovakia. Hitler was wild with self-satisfaction, exclaiming gleefully to his secretaries: "Children, this is the greatest day of my life. I shall go down in history as the greatest German." And had he died of apoplexy on the spot, he might well have been right. In four and a half years he had taken a chaotic, powerless Germany and lifted her up to challenge the old world powers, Britain and France. His wild speeches, his anti-Semitism, his *Mein Kampf* pledges of world conquest might have been passed over in later years as a young politician's excesses.

This was not to be. Six years of life remained to the Führer and he had already made a big mistake. In time he might have absorbed Czechoslovakia. But to have so quickly violated his Munich promises extinguished the last naïve trust in his word of honor. Even Chamberlain would not be duped again. The goodwill and patience of the Western powers had been overly abused, though not until March 31 did Chamberlain speak out: "In the event of any action which clearly threatens Polish independence and which the Polish government accordingly considered it vital to resist with their national forces, His Majesty's government would feel themselves bound at once to lend the Polish Government all support in their power."

But Hitler was in high gear. His Machiavellian sense of timing at playing one nation against another was giving way to blind avariciousness. Already the Polish ambassador in Berlin was being approached about a comprehensive settlement of German-Polish problems. The cycle of conquest was beginning again, but this time there would be war—war with forty-three million corpses, nearly half of them Russian; over six million Poles, Germans, and Jews; two million Yugoslavs; nearly a million French; half a million Americans and British; and hundreds of thousands of gypsies not to mention lesser numbers of countless other nationalities.

POLAND'S TURN: 1939

In *Mein Kampf,* Hitler had not concerned himself with the Poles. He considered them an inferior people, inconveniently occupying territory between Germany and *Lebensraum* in Russia. After World War I Poland had been granted a corridor to the sea which separated East Prussia from the bulk of Germany, and the formerly German port of Danzig had been made a free state. In the autumn of 1938 Hitler had begun complaining about this situation, and on April 3, 1939, he introduced his generals to a secret "Case White," which set out plans for conquering Poland. September 1 was the target date. Two days before, with typical cynicism, he had announced for September the Nazi Party Convention for Peace.

At this time Hitler could do no wrong in Germany. For his fiftieth birthday, on April 20, schoolchildren all over Germany sang the following:

Adolf Hitler is our savior, our hero.
He is the noblest being in the whole wide world.
For Hitler we live.
For Hitler we die.
Our Hitler is our Lord,
Who rules a brave New World.

Such extravagant tributes were eroding away his Machiavellian calculations. He, too, saw himself as superhuman. He would have Poland. The usual propaganda pressure began building up but the Poles were a determined people. They would not submit to words and they had England's pledge of support. The lines were drawn, though Hitler still suspected that, faced with an accomplished fact, the British would once again back off.

The key to the situation seemed to be the Soviet Union, Poland's eastern neighbor and friend to neither fascist Germany nor capitalist England. Yet whoever first obtained Russian allegiance would command the situation. While a suspicious Anglo-French delegation took six days to go to Russia by slow cargo ship and train, the Germans resorted to airplanes and telegrams and on August 23 signed a nonaggression pact with Russia. Hitler, having evidently forgotten his prediction in *Mein Kampf* that such a treaty would inevitably bring "the end of Germany" was delighted. Poland was isolated.

Early on the morning of August 24, 1939, Hitler was still celebrating at his mountainside Berghof when the sky turned crimson with the northern lights. "The last act of *Götterdämmer-*

ung [Wagner's opera *Twilight of the Gods*]," said one guest. "A great deal of blood," observed Hitler. "This time we won't make it without violence." Three days later he canceled the Party rally for peace. World War II was about to begin.

Until the end Hitler kept up a veneer of negotiation. Even after the final attack order had been secretly given, he had prepared a seemingly reasonable sixteen-point proposal to the Poles. Though it was never, in fact, presented, German radio stations would suggest after war had begun that the Poles had rejected it, thereby pushing the war guilt upon them. Other elaborate tricks were concocted to make Case White seem a Polish aggression. Most notorious was "Operation Canned Goods" which called for a phony SS attack on the German radio station at Gleiwitz near the Polish boarder. For realism a number of drugged concentration camp inmates were stuffed into Polish uniforms, taken to the radio station area, and shot as though killed in battle, while German radio blared out toward dawn on September 1: "This night for the first time Polish regular soldiers fired on our territory. Since five forty-five A.M. we have been returning the fire."

Next morning at the Kroll Opera House, Hitler addressed the Reichstag, saying: "I am from now on just the first soldier of the German Reich. I have once more donned that coat which was most sacred and precious to me. I will not take it off again until victory is secured or I will not survive the outcome." Figuratively, at least, he spoke the truth for once. No longer was he weighing political alternatives. From now on he was obsessed with military objectives.

Sunday, September 3, dawned clear and hot. Berliners were already seeking relief in the nearby lakes and woods when at 9:00 A.M. the British ambassador called at Ribbentrop's office. Suspecting the worst, Ribbentrop left the dirty work to his interpreter Paul Schmidt, who carried the message to Hitler. It was a declaration of war. "What next?" Hitler wondered, and Ribbentrop was there to tell him, "I presume that the French will hand in a similar ultimatum within the hour." Even for Hitler this was a solemn moment, but Göring summed it up most succinctly: "If we lose this war, then God have pity on us."

Polish cavalry charged German tanks with lowered lances.

It was a slaughter. The outcome was clear within five days and on September 17, like a vulture to the carrion feast, came Russia. Meanwhile, France, burdened with the ghastly memories of World War I, was slow to mobilize. England, despite its firmer resolve, had the channel to cross. Even a modest attack in the west at this time might have caused Germany's defeat, but it did not come.

Once again Hitler had correctly judged his enemies. Had they attacked, Germany was in no position to carry on a protracted war of attrition. That had been the pattern of World War I and Hitler would have none of it. His whole strategy was to pick off one enemy at a time with *"Blitzkrieg"* (lightening warfare) attacks. German industry lacked the capacity to do otherwise, needing an interval between each campaign to stockpile armaments. Ammunition had almost entirely been spent in Poland. Against one enemy at a time, Germany could throw the best-trained, most modern army in the world, but if ever opposed by a stubborn coalition dedicated to a long wasteful war, she was doomed.

THE PHONY WAR

In the beginning the British and French seemed content to abide by Hitler's rules. In mid-October, three weeks after Poland had fallen, England had managed to move a token four divisions to France, and German radio was propagandizing: "Why do France and England want to fight now? Germany wants nothing in the west." There was a tinge of sincerity in this appeal, which was totally expunged by Chamberlain's House of Commons speech on October 12. No reliance could be put on the promises of the present German government, he said. If it seriously craved peace "acts not words alone must be forthcoming." Chamberlain was no longer Hitler's dupe, and accusing England of prolonging the war, the führer began planning his attack in the west. Fearful of another two-front war, he had to overcome England and France before tackling the real foe, Russia. Week by week his attack was postponed. Instead, French troops were showered with leaflets showing themselves shivering at the front while English soldiers cavorted with their wives back home. This was the *Sitzkrieg* ("the phony war") but it did allow the German forces time to rearm.

On November 30, 1939, the Soviets attacked Finland, a close friend of Germany. Hitler seethed. He was not ready for a two-front war and he needed Russian raw materials which otherwise had been cut off by the British blockade, materials for a spring campaign in the west.

NORWAY AND DENMARK

It was Russia's conduct that led to code name "Weser Exercise," the subjugation of Norway and Denmark, beginning on April 9, 1940. Both were Nordic people, neutrals in World War I, and Hitler would have left them alone except that, with Russia in Finland, England had an excuse to move troops to Norway, thereby outflanking Germany in the north.

In Denmark, the German foreign minister presented an ultimatum that they accept immediate "protection from the Reich," and before most Danes had risen from the breakfast table, Denmark had submitted. However, Norway, with its population of only three million, announced: "We will not submit voluntarily. The struggle is already under way." By noon, five major Norwegian cities were in German hands. Still, the fight lingered on. The Norwegians gallantly resolved upon guerrilla warfare, and with the belated aid of Britain, they inflicted losses upon the German navy from which it would never entirely recover.

WAR IN THE WEST

Another military success only confirmed Hitler's rejection of the old political methods at which he had so excelled. "Politics?" he said once. "I don't engage in politics anymore. All that disgusts me so." And strictly speaking he never took part in politics again. His mood was visionary, Siegfried marching to victory. And in many ways his judgments were foresighted and bold. His generals favored the World War I plan of sending a curving attack through the Low Countries (Belgium, Luxembourg, and the Netherlands) into France, but Hitler embraced the idea of striking with armor straight through the Ardennes forest. This strategy would work well, but in time his strength would erode, boldness becoming recklessness, inexhaustibility hardening into rigidity. But his failures as commander in chief were far in the future when, in the early dawn of May 10, 1940, the representatives of Belgium and Holland were informed by Ribbentrop that German armies had already entered their lands to save them from attack by the English and French. This was not the main assault, but it succeeded in luring the French and English armies to combat and entrapment after the main thrust struck like an avalanche through the Ardennes.

Holland and Belgium fell within days. The demoralized French army never seriously resisted. Within two weeks the British expeditionary force, along with numerous French soldiers, were trapped along the Channel coast. Four panzer (tank) divisions were closing in for the kill when, to their amazement, they were ordered to halt. The job of finishing off the Allied armies was left to the Luftwaffe (The German Air Force). The result was that, by June 4, over 300,000 soldiers had been evacuated to England. For the most part, Luftwaffe bombs had muffled themselves in the sand, for the English it was a miracle in their darkest hour, and why Hitler let it happen remains a question: Was it to give some glory to Göring's pilots? To spare a beaten foe who would inevitably sue for peace? Hitler's own explanation was placatory. "Churchill," he said, "was quite unable to appreciate the sporting spirit of which I had given proof by refraining from creating an irreparable breach between the British and ourselves."

Whatever the reason, Hitler had reached high tide. He had forged ahead to victory where many of his generals had predicted disaster. On June 21, at the cost of only twenty-seven thousand casualties, he brought once-proud France to her knees. On that day armistice negotiations began. Hitler had erased the stain of Versailles and he rode in triumph through the streets of Berlin. It was the last time he would do so.

ENGLAND THE ENIGMA

But the defeated and perplexed English didn't seem to know they were beaten. Their new prime minister Winston Churchill was promising victory. "In this hour I feel it to be my duty before my own conscience to appeal once more to reason and common sense in Great Britain as much as elsewhere. I consider myself in a position to make this appeal since I am not the vanquished begging favors but the victor speaking in the name of reason."

Half-heartedly, during the summer of 1940 Hitler began planning "Operation Sea Lion." "Sailing against England" became a popular song, but England was still protected by the finest navy in the world. The only hope was for the Luftwaffe to dominate the skies, and throughout August and early September they battled the British fighter planes and suffered staggering losses. Operation Sea Lion was postponed, and as autumn advanced, Hitler began to see victory slipping from his fingers and into an endless stalemate with a country he had never been anxious to fight, while the Soviet Union, the real foe, fattened itself in the east. His alternatives were to build up ties with Japan and the Soviet Union against the British Empire with her growing support from the United States, a path of concession which would endlessly delay his reckoning with Russia; or to strike suddenly at Russia, defeating her as he had done the others with a motorized *Blitzkrieg,* and then turn back to face England with his own power block composed of slaves, not demanding partners. He chose the latter alternative, for it involved quick solutions, *Lebensraum,* and the destruction of communist Jews.

In late July 1940 he had already consulted his reluctant general staff about attacking Russia. This would be the two-front war they all feared. England should be vanquished first, but with the September failure to invade the British Isles, Hitler's mind was made up. In the spring Russia would be crushed.

Intervening were months of frustration. There were negotiations with Spain's General Francisco Franco over the possible seizure of Gibraltar, which would have sealed off the British fleet from the Mediterranean; but Franco never would come to terms, largely for a personal reason unknown to Hitler. Franco had Jewish blood. There were the bunglings of Mussolini, who attacked tiny Greece on October 28. "Why on earth," Hitler lamented, "didn't Mussolini attack Malta or Crete," which would have helped in the war with England for the Mediterranean. Even in Greece the Italians faltered against Greece's diminutive but plucky army. The attack on Russia was to begin in May, but the Italian debacle in Greece, together with an uprising of Yugoslav army officers against a pact with Germany, led to a four-week postponement. Hitler could not chance the possibility of English intervention on the mainland, so twenty-nine German divisions rolled into Greece. Three weeks in April did the job with the strategic island of Crete falling in late May. Here was a golden opportunity. As Admiral Erich Raeder, who had never liked the idea of attacking Russia, saw it, Hitler should move on against Egypt and the Suez Canal. "Such a stroke would be more deadly to the British Empire than the capture of London," Raeder pleaded, and he was very probably right. Hitler would not listen.

For months Soviet intelligence had been predicting the attack. Stalin could not believe Hitler would be that foolish, with England still a threat. Nor had victory given Germany valuable allies. Japan was too far away to help and had declined to stab Russia in the back. Italy and Spain were unreliable at best, as was the puppet government at Vichy which administered that portion of France not officially under German occupation.

LEBENSRAUM IN RUSSIA

Against the immensity of Russia, Hitler's only hope was to attract the millions of Russians who hated Stalin's communism. Hitler had no such practical intentions. The Russian campaign was to be merciless. "The commissars are the bearers of ideologies directly opposed to National Socialism," he said. "Therefore the commissars will be liquidated. German soldiers guilty of breaking international law . . . will be excused. Russia has not participated in the Hague convention and therefore has no rights under it." Conquered territory would be scoured for the necessities of life. If millions of peasants starved as a result, so much the better; their removal would contribute to more living space.

The attack was set for 3:30 A.M., June 22, 1941. For the benefit of the German public, the impending attack was hastily being justified by reports of Russian espionage and terrorism. Three million soldiers waited meanwhile along a nine-hundred-mile front that fateful night of June 21 as their commanders read out Hitler's encouraging words: "German soldiers! You are about to join battle, a hard and crucial battle. The destiny of Europe and future of our nation now lie in your hands alone." As midnight approached, a last unwitting freight train carrying Russian grain to Germany chugged over the frontier. Three hours and fifteen minutes later the attack began with the firing of over 7,000 cannon and spearheaded by 3,580 tanks, the most awesome army ever to take part in a single assault. As Hitler recalled, it was the same day in June that Napoleon crossed the Niemen River on his way to Moscow.

In Germany the attack, of course, was blamed on Russia, with Goebbels proclaiming: "Now that the Führer has unmasked the treachery of the Bolshevik rulers, National Socialism and hence the German people are reverting to the principles which impelled them—the struggle against plutocracy and Bolshevism." He concluded by reducing Hitler's forecast of victory in four months to only eight weeks.

With the attack well under way, Hitler moved from Berlin to a forest headquarters in East Prussia, called Wolf's Lair. Victory seemed at hand. "How lucky it was that we smashed the Russian armor and air force right in the beginning," he gloated. "In several weeks we will be in Moscow. There is no doubt of it. I will raze the damned city and I will build an artificial lake with central lighting in its place. The name of Moscow will disappear forever."

But the Russians, despite incredible casualties, fought doggedly. It was do or die against Hitler's policies of *Lebensraum* and annihilation. As the summer progressed and the far-flung assault diffused into the vastness of Russia, the army high command urged a concentration on Moscow. It was the transportation hub and armament center; around their sacred capital the last Russian armies could be expected to stand and die, after which the nation's spirit would be broken. Hitler wanted more, the Ukrainian breadbasket and the oil fields of the Caucasus. His military genius seemed confirmed when 665,000 Russian prisoners were taken at Kiev, but two months of good weather had been squandered and not until October of 1941 did the assault on Moscow begin.

By this time Russia was turning cold and German armies prepared only for the summer *Blitzkrieg* had no winter clothes or equipment. The spires of Moscow had been glimpsed by Hitler's first line of attack but autumn mud, ice, and subzero cold brought an end to the advance. By December 6 the irresistible army was withdrawing under suicidally brave Russian counterattacks. The consummate politician was showing weaknesses as a war leader, but typically he blamed his generals, and on December 9 he announced that he was taking over command of the army directly. This represented his complete triumph over the Prussian officer corps, but it was his only victory during December, and it was the beginning of the end. Not only had his unbeatable army been stopped but, on the other side of the world, on December 7 at Pearl Harbor, the United States had been drawn into the war, the long war on more than two fronts which Germany had not intended and which she could not hope to win.

ACT V:
GÖTTERDÄMMERUNG
FOR THE NEW ORDER,
1942–45

PLAN FOR THE NEW WORLD ORDER

Hitler had grown up believing that life was a struggle for existence between animals, men, and nations. "One being drinks the blood of another. By dying, the one furnishes food for the other. We should not blather about humanity," he had written. The one racial group that stood above the inferior masses was the Aryan, "the Promethean bearers of light," as some called them. In the mid-1920s Hitler had recorded these views in *Mein Kampf,* and in 1939 he began waging that "racial" struggle beyond German frontiers.

Nazism regarded the rest of the world as a kind of livestock farm, and it is perhaps appropriate that the man in charge of the "animals" was a former poultry farmer, Heinrich Himmler, who undertook the elimination of inferior races as dispassionately as that farmer would breed out inferior chickens. Similarly, his SS officers who manned the gas chambers could do so dutifully, relaxing after a day of slaughter with untroubled hearts. So widely believed were these racial fantasies that the high command of the armed forces could issue the following policy statement: "For reasons of racial hygiene, it is undesirable to use prisoners of war as blood donors for members of the German folk community, because we cannot be sure that no men of mixed Jewish blood among the prisoners would be used for blood donations."

In theory, at least, the new world order would recognize Germany as the capital over all. From this center, SS concentrations—half garrisons, half monasteries in keeping with the religious order of Knight Templars who garrisoned areas of the Holy Land during and after the crusades—would radiate out to maintain the Nazi peace as the Templars had pledged to keep the peace of God among the infidels. Through them a refreshing of the population's blood would be provided. Jews would be eliminated, Slavic inferiors gradually supplanted by a wave of Aryan settlers. As Martin Bormann, Hitler's secretary, wrote, on July 23, 1942, "The Slavs are to work for us. In so far as we don't need them, they may die." In ten years, Hitler envisioned, at least ten million Germans would be living in the conquered East.

THE NEW ORDER IN APPLICATION

When German troops first marched into Russia, they were often greeted as liberators, though already in conquered Poland the new order had initiated the elimination of Jews and intellectuals and the savage exploitation of Polish raw materials, factories, and even art treasures.

As the German armies ravaged further east, they were followed by four SS *Einsatzgruppen* ("task forces"), consisting of 3,000 men each, whose purpose it was to secure occupied territory and liquidate Asiatic inferiors, the incurably ill, Bolshevik leaders, Jews, and Gypsies. Himmler's first deputy in this project was Reinhard Heydrich and under Heydrich was an officers' corps, for the most part made up of efficient young professional men—former lawyers, doctors, even a Protestant pastor—who brought their training and talents to the task of mass execution, the so-called final solution of the Jewish problem.

The final solution had long been in Hitler's mind and he gave voice to such an undertaking as early as January 30,

1939, in a speech to the Reichstag: "If the international Jewish financiers . . . should again succeed in plunging the nations into world war the result will be . . . the annihilation of the Jewish race throughout Europe." Not until March 31, 1941, did Hitler's decision for mass execution take concrete form, when he spoke to a number of generals about Himmler's "special tasks" behind the fighting front. On July 31, 1941, Heydrich received the obscure command "to make all necessary preparations for organization and financial matters to bring about a final solution of the Jewish problem in the German sphere of influence in Europe."

Hitler had long admired the British "concentration camps" for Boer prisoners in South Africa and the efficient reservation system in the United States where red savages dwindled through starvation and disease. Conquered Poland was chosen as the site for his new extermination camps, and before they were put out of business, some six million Jews and countless other "inferiors" would die there.

Despite Nazi doctrine describing how internationally well organized was the world "Jewish conspiracy," the truth was otherwise. The Soviet press had scarcely mentioned Hitler's anti-Semitic actions before the invasion and many Russian Jews greeted the advancing Germans as liberators. They were for the most part completely unprepared, and as fundamentally peaceful people accustomed to age-old persecution, they accepted the "Jewish councils" as buffers through which to work with the Germans. These councils, nominally run by leaders of the Jewish community with the express goal of easing the relationship between the Jews and their Nazi oppressors, inevitably became the helpless tools of the SS in unwittingly expediting the removal of Jews to the death camps.

Initially, extermination was a haphazard affair carried out by firing squads. Himmler, the only high-ranking Nazi to witness such a spectacle, nearly fainted, and it was partly due to his "humane nature" that in the future extermination was done "mercifully." Mercy meant efficiency in this case, and efficiency meant gas. Hitler was receptive to this idea. He had tasted gas in 1918 and in *Mein Kampf* had advocated its use upon Jewish corrupters of the German people.

Only Hitler could have been responsible for making the final solution a reality. To him it was as vital as *Lebensraum,* an unavoidable prerequisite to building "something wonderfully beautiful," and with insane missionary zeal he continued detailing trains for carrying Jews to death camps in Poland, ironically trains which otherwise could have been used to supply his increasingly hard-pressed armies. Perhaps there was a conscience locked in him somewhere, for he never observed a single execution and could scarcely have comprehended the horror that was his doing. This same psychotic split personality imbued the entire program, and as much as possible the German public was isolated from the truth. Jewish neighbors simply disappeared, presumably to be settled elsewhere, and as the secret began to escape, it was easier to denounce it as Allied propaganda than as the monstrous truth.

So, through 1943 the Polish extermination camps operated at peak efficiency, until the outcome of the war was in doubt; with reduced German manpower, it became more important to work the inmates as long as they had the strength. From then on, only the physically unfit went to the gas chambers. In the end, with the new order collapsing, there was an effort to eradicate the camps, the *Totenbuchs* ("death books"), and the dead, but the crime against humanity was too monumental, and it is burned into the record of civilization as Hitler's most demonic achievement. The new order he imagined is all but forgotten.

DEFEAT BECOMES INEVITABLE

At first Hitler had conscientiously avoided conflict with the United States. He feared its industrial potential, but at the same time despised American leadership as a "Jewish clique." By the summer of 1941 he was saying, "I am of the opinion that we [Germany and Japan] must jointly destroy them," and his reaction to the Japanese attack on the U.S. naval base at Pearl Harbor on December 7, 1941, was one of complete joy. "We cannot lose the war," he exclaimed, and on the eleventh of December he declared war on the United States. By this time his exuberance had cooled. In one stroke the attack on Pearl Harbor had relieved Russia of the fear of a Japanese attack in the east, raised battered Britain's determination to hold out, and galvanized the world's greatest industrial power to crush the Axis. This impact was soon felt. Under American initiative the Allies—the United States, Britain, and Russia—began coordinating their efforts via numerous conferences into the single goal of defeating the enemy, a unity of purpose never achieved by Germany, Italy, and Japan.

American aid to Britain was evidenced as early as May 3, 1942, when the Royal Air Force achieved its first one-thousand-plane raid. In fact that night 1,130 planes dropped bombs on Cologne and that was just the beginning. On October 23 a beefed up British army in North Africa finally turned the tide against Hitler's Africa Corps at Alamein. Two weeks later General Dwight D. Eisenhower was landing American troops in Morocco and Algeria. Despite Hitler's command to General Erwin Rommel not to fall back "one inch, triumph or die," the Nazi adventure in the Mediterranean that might have strangled the British Empire was crumbling, and thanks to this no-retreat order, 300,000 German and Italian troops would be captured in Tunisia.by the spring of 1943.

The Mediterranean had always been of secondary interest to Hitler. Russia constantly obsessed him, and following reversals in the snows of 1941 and 1942, a renewed summer offensive had raised his hopes and led him once again into the error of a split offensive—Army Group A to advance on Rostov and the Black Sea, Group B to march on Stalingrad. When his generals objected, he simply told General Franz Halder, "We need National Socialist ardor now, not professional ability. I cannot expect this of an officer of the old school such as you." By autumn the German Sixth Army had finally reached Stalingrad. Reports of a massive Soviet buildup were repudiated as his high command's typical overestimation of the enemy. Then on November 19, 1942, forty Russian divisions struck the long extended flank of the German advance at a portion held by reluctant Romanian allies. Though begged by his generals to call for the Sixth Army to withdraw in late December, Hitler would have none of it. "No matter what happens, we must hold the area around Stalingrad," he said. As matters worsened, Hitler withdrew more and more from his advisers, keeping company only with his dog, Blondi. At the end of 1943 the Sixth Army survivors surrendered. With Stalingrad, German initiative in the east ended. By November of 1943, Germany had suffered over 1.5 million casualties in a single year. Only the young and old remained to be drafted, and matters could go only from bad to worse.

Meanwhile, in the Mediterranean the situation was also deteriorating. On July 10, 1943, the Allies invaded Sicily. With this, Mussolini's fascist lieutenants began demanding his resignation and a restoration of King Victor Emmanuel. On the 25th the king actually dismissed the tottering Il Duce, and Marshal Pietro Badoglio formed a nonparty government in the hope of getting in touch with the Allies. When on September 3 the Allies finally invaded the Italian mainland the new Italian regime announced that an armistice was being signed with the Western Allies. All this Hitler had anticipated. German troops invaded Italy from the north and on September 12 Mussolini was rescued from custody. Though broken in spirit, Mussolini would be propped up by Hitler as a puppet leader of fascist Italy in the north. From this point onward German troops occupied and governed Italy, and until the end made a hard fight to hold this second front against the dogged wasting onslaught of the Allies.

A third front was expected any day in France, and troops otherwise needed to hold off the Russians were delegated to build an "Atlantic wall" against a seaborne attack from England. It did not come until June 6, 1944, at which point the Allies had what Hitler never achieved for his abortive Operation Sea Lion: complete mastery of the skies. When the first landings came, the German command could not decide if it was the real thing or a diversion. Hitler was not at first awakened and when he was, he concluded the Normandy landing was a fake and withheld freedom of action from his field commanders to converge on the beaches. By midnight, at the cost of twenty-five hundred lives, the Allies had opened a thirty-mile front in Hitler's *Festung Europa* ("Fortress Europe"). By that time the battle was lost, and Hitler's only spiteful recourse was the launching on June 12 of V-1 rockets against

London. These, Hitler insisted, followed by masses of jet fighters would turn the tide; meanwhile, his harassed armies were told to hold every inch of ground.

July 20, 1944, brought a massive Russian offensive which would soon push into Poland. On the same day, a clique of army officers tried to assassinate Hitler with a bomb. Hitler survived, only to exult to his secretaries, "Well, my ladies. . . . More proof that fate has selected me for my mission. Otherwise I wouldn't be alive," and he sent his bomb-tattered uniform to his mistress Eva Braun as proof of divine intercession. Congratulations poured into his headquarters, for the vast majority of Germans still felt, as Hitler did, that the nation's future depended on his leadership alone.

HITLER AS WAR LEADER

Hitler had proved himself a Machiavellian politician and diplomat. The bold first military campaigns had seemed to confirm his soldierly talents as well. On April 24, 1942, he compared himself favorably to Napoleon, saying, "We have mastered destiny, which broke another man a hundred and thirty years ago." At the same time, he assumed direct powers of life and death over every German, who henceforth would be subject to his personal commands. Yet all the while he was withdrawing. He spoke less often in public. Physically he was deteriorating, with shoulders hunched and feet dragging. Gradually, his fixed opinions took absolute precedence over cold reality. Formerly, contempt for reality had been a bold tool, but now he seldom emerged from headquarters, and could not confront wounded soldiers. So as not to witness the ravages caused by Allied bombers, he seldom traveled and then only in a train with blinds drawn.

As reality escaped him, his military judgment became more and more rigid. In December 1941 when Field Marshal Fedor von Bock, commander of the central front in Russia, sought permission to withdraw, Hitler sacked him and assumed personal command of the army. The only sort of general he could endure for long were the toadish ones such as Generals Wilhelm Keitel and Alfred Jodl, and thus he closed himself off further from expert and contradictory opinion. When strategic withdrawal or annihilation became the alternative, holding out to the last man remained his rule, and so at Stalingrad and in North Africa irreplaceable armies were sacrificed. Though in 1943 German armies still comprised nine million men, they were scattered over half a continent, holding a great and leaking bag without any thought to what was essential, what expendable.

Hitler's survival of the July 20, 1944, bomb plot not only seemed to confirm his providential mission, it focused past failures upon the traitors among his officers. Total war was henceforth decreed, under the slogan, "The people want it." Furloughs were canceled, places of entertainment shut down. Still, matters went from bad to worse. The very next day Paris was liberated. Former allies Romania and Hungary sued for peace. Hitler's faith grasped at straws. Like Frederick the Great, he would snatch victory from defeat. As his energies flagged, his voice growing faint and his hands trembling, his body was sustained by drugs which seemed to draw on what might be called life for years in advance—every year Hitler aged not a year but four or five.

Still, he maintained his hypnotic power over the German people to the end, not the exuberant faith of old but a dull sense of being tied to Hitler in destiny. Never did he seriously consider capitulation. As early as February 1945 he told the Propaganda Ministry to insult the Allied leaders so that they would not be willing to tempt Germany with offers short of complete surrender. If they held out past endurance, until "after midnight" as Hitler liked to phrase it, without crumbling as had been the case in World War I, victory would come as it had to Frederick the Great, who despairingly had spoken of killing himself on February 15, 1762. "Brave king wait yet a little while and the days of your suffering will be over," Carlyle had advised him, and three days before the appointed suicide the czarina Elizabeth of Russia had died and Prussia was subsequently spared ignominious defeat. Hitler, too, need only hold out and providence would save the day; for this fancy, hundreds of thousands more would die in the last weeks of World War II.

NAZISM IN DEFEAT

Armaments production in Germany was never higher than in 1944, but the means of continuing the war were beginning to cancel each other out. Thirty-eight thousand planes were built but lacked the fuel to take off. Millions of shells were manufactured, but their explosive contents were being padded with 20 percent salt.

By September 11 the first American patrols stood on German soil in the west. Russians were massing on the border of East Prussia. Still, Hitler had one last throw of the dice. To attack the Russians he might delay the end, but to assault the British and Americans might split their coalition, and with that nostalgia which often influenced Hitler's decisions, he envisioned a thrust once more through the Ardennes where the British and American forces met. On December 16, 1944, the surprise attack was launched. Hitler pictured it rolling to the sea. "We gamble everything. You carry with you the holy obligation to give all to achieve superhuman objectives for our Fatherland and our Führer," Field Marshal Karl von Rundstedt told his troops, in words reminiscent of the attack on Russia three and a half years before. By January 16, 1945, the Battle of the Bulge was over, with heavy loses on both sides. The Allies could afford them; Hitler could not, for a Russian offensive had already begun in the east.

On January 30, 1945, the anniversary of his becoming chancellor, Hitler made his last public speech. "I never wanted to fight the West. . . . they forced it on me," he said, but Germany must hold out against the "Asian tidal wave," since "time is our ally." In the end the Western capitalists would surely battle the Russian communists. It was only a matter of time. Meanwhile, Hitler withdrew to his Berlin bunker, planned a remodeled city of Linz, listened morbidly to the *Götterdämmerung* on the phonograph, and forbade contact with the enemy. "Whoever talks to the enemy is a traitor to the idea. We may fall in the fight against Bolshevism but we shall not negotiate with it."

Yet even in the back of Hitler's mind clearly lurked the specter of defeat, not abject surrender but that *Götterdämmerung* worthy of gods; the great catastrophe to carry him out of this world. To that end, on March 19 he ordered all military transportation, all communications, supplies, and industry to be destroyed, not to mention monuments, castles, churches, and opera houses. Nothing was to be left with which the German people could survive. Of course, in the growing chaos this command was impossible to implement, and was further blocked by Hitler's architect friend and minister of armaments, Albert Speer, who countermanded the orders when he could.

Otherwise, Hitler's authority remained strong until the last. Though he then lacked power to punish, somehow his subordinates stayed obedient to his will. On April 20, 1945, his fifty-sixth birthday, Goebbels, Himmler, Ribbentrop, Göring, and others were dutifully on hand. With Berlin being encircled, it seemed high time for Hitler to withdraw to a last Alpine redoubt, but he would not budge. Others fled the doomed city. Cut off from the rest of Germany by all but radio, Hitler's personality still commanded the last battle.

LAST WILL AND TESTAMENT

Hitler had threatened suicide before. As Germany dwindled throughout April of 1945, that threat was nearing reality. His bunker at Berchtesgaden would be a tomb or the citadel of miraculous victory. On April 16 another death brought him absurd hope. Like the czarina, Roosevelt had died. Briefly the Nazis celebrated this evident turn of the tide, but the war went on as before. Three days later Russian troops opened their final assault on the city, and by April 29 hope was given up. A local magistrate was called in to marry Hitler and Eva Braun. Was this a touch of humanity showing through—the neglected Eva had longed to be his wife—or was it simply abdication? As a leader he had belonged only to Germany. Whatever the motive, it was a gruesome death pact acted out with cakes and wine.

The next day Hitler was saying, "I want them to write on

my tombstone, 'He was the victim of his generals.' " Even in these last hours Hitler remained unchanged, blameless, the betrayed savior of his people. It is all recorded in his political and private testaments. From the former come the following conclusions:

> It is untrue that I or anybody else in Germany wanted war in 1939. It was wanted and provoked exclusively by those international statesmen who either were of Jewish origin or worked for Jewish interest. . . . The people and the armed forces have given their all in this long hard struggle, the struggle has been enormous but my trust has been misused by many people, disloyalty and betrayal have undermined resistance throughout the war. It was therefore not granted to me to lead the people to victory. The army general staff cannot be compared with the general staff in the first world war. Its achievements were far behind those of the fighting front. . . . Above all, I enjoin the government and the people to uphold the racial laws to the limit and to resist mercilessly the poisoner of all nations, international Jewry.

In conclusion he sang the same old song: "The efforts and sacrifices of the German people in this war have been so great that I cannot believe that they have been in vain. The aim must still be to win territory in the east for the German people."

His personal testament was far briefer, but kept his fantasies intact by leaving his art treasures to a proposed gallery in Linz. At 4:00 A.M. on April 29 the two documents were signed. Hitler was finally ready to die. Shortly after three o'clock the following afternoon he took leave of his aides, then with his wife retired to his quarters where he sat down facing his mother's portrait. A single shot rang out. Eva had taken poison.

Unbending adolescent to the end, Hitler had been chancellor for twelve years and three months. His thousand-year Reich would outlive him by a week. His burial place was to have been the bell tower of a mighty monument, but in fact his corpse was lowered into a Russian shell hole outside the bunker entrance. So thoroughly did the gasoline fire devour his remains that many continued to believe him alive, perhaps on a remote island, in a Spanish monastery or Argentine hacienda. In life Hitler's successes had been largely the result of his enemies' mistakes. Now typical Russian unwillingness to share its secrets gave him rumored life after death until 1972, when they finally released human remains which allowed a dental comparison to prove conclusively that Adolf Hitler had really died in Berlin.

THE END

On May 7, 1945, Admiral Karl Doenitz, as Hitler's deputy, signaled General Eisenhower that he would sign an unconditional surrender. At midnight on May 8 the guns fell silent. The Third Reich was vanquished. The atomic bomb has made another conqueror in the mold of Alexander the Great or Napoleon unlikely. Though Hitler often compared himself with these two, he left little but desolation—no surviving ideas such as the Code Napoleon or the spread of Greek culture to the east. But he had reshaped the map of Europe, destroyed empires, ended Western Europe's colonial era, and inadvertently produced a double irony, the westward extension of communism and the formation of a Jewish state.

Though Hitler's only legacy was death, destruction, and abiding shame, it cannot be doubted that while he lived, his people worshiped him more unhesitatingly than they had Martin Luther or Frederick the Great. With him went National Socialism, vanishing like a sorcerer's evil spell. In 1918 the monarchy collapsed and the emperor fled, but the institution of the state and the core of the army had remained. In the spring of 1945 the Third Reich melted away. A regime that had depended on force and personality had no institutions left, no vitality to resist "soulless" American capitalism on the one hand or Russian communism on the other. How ironic then that a nation emptied of ideology should today be split between these two camps.

There is a new pragmatic generation in Germany today. Hitler had no future vision but ruled by the force of his voice, and when that voice was stilled, no guiding principles remained. What he did do was amputate the past, and any withdrawal into Prussian militarism was cut off. In 1945 West Germany did not turn inward, but began an almost complete about-face toward the West. Militarism became repulsive, the army an organization of low regard. This change of attitude was largely fostered by a more farsighted postwar policy than the one that rejected Germany after World War I. Hitler would have little appeal in a prospering country wallowing in the good things of consumer capitalism.

Could Nazism happen again? German universities remain centers of unrest, but the last likelihood seems to be another Hitler. For the most part, Germany is a burned-out crater of big-power politics. She has no stab-in-the-back legend, no "Jewish conspiracy" myth to spur her on. In fact, if democracy should falter, the greatest probability is that it will be supplanted by communism, that totalitarian system which exists in East Germany and which, although Nazism's undying foe, is more akin to Nazism in practice than to democracy.

And elsewhere? To expect a duplication of National Socialism at some future time in some other place would be to deny the fact of perpetual change; but to deny that peoples will again be galvanized by some messianic cause would be to deny the lessons of history. Whatever lessons were taught by Nazism, however, are elementary at best: that a nation should never let itself be driven to desperation by its neighbors, that power should not be placed in the hands of the young or emotionally unstable, that a voting public must remain objective and well informed. These are trivial suggestions perhaps, but the fact remains that, though Hitler is dead and his ashes scattered, his spirit lingers, waiting to invest itself in other demagogues, and other overwrought peoples willing to be led to the slaughter.

BIBLIOGRAPHY

Allen, William S. *The Nazi Seizure of Power.* Chicago: Quadrangle Books, 1965.

Bezymenski, Lev. *The Death of Adolf Hitler.* New York: Harcourt, Brace & World, 1968.

Bleuel, Hans P. *Sex and Society in Nazi Germany.* Philadelphia: Lippincott, 1973.

Blond, Georges. *The Death of Hitler's Germany.* New York: Macmillan, 1954.

Boldt, Gerhard. *Hitler: The Last Ten Days.* New York: Coward, McCann, & Geoghegan, 1973.

Bracher, Karl D. *The German Dictatorship.* New York: Praeger, 1970.

Breiting, Richard. *Secret Conversations with Hitler.* New York: John Day, 1971.

Brissaud, André. *The Nazi Secret Service.* New York: Norton, 1974.

Bullock, Alan L. *Hitler: A Study in Tyranny.* New York: Harper & Row, 1962.

Compton, James V. *The Swastika and the Eagle.* Boston: Houghton Mifflin, 1967.

Conway, J. S. *The Nazi Persecution of the Churches, 1933–45.* New York: Basic Books, 1968.

Crankshaw, Edward. *Gestapo.* New York: Viking Press, 1956.

Deakin, Frederick W. *The Brutal Friendship: Mussolini, Hitler, and the Fall of Italian Fascism.* New York: Harper & Row, 1962.

Delarue, Jacques. *The Gestapo.* New York: Morrow, 1964.

Donohoe, James. *Hitler's Conservative Opponents in Bavaria.* Leiden, Netherlands: E. J. Brill, 1961.

Elliott, Brendan J. *Hitler and Germany.* New York: McGraw-Hill, 1968.

Eyck, Erich. *A History of the Weimar Republic.* New York: Atheneum, 1962.

Fest, Joachim C. *The Face of the Third Reich.* New York: Pantheon Books, 1970.

————. *Hitler.* New York: Harcourt Brace Jovanovich, 1974.

Fireside, Harvey. *Icon and Swastika.* Cambridge, Mass.: Harvard University Press, 1971.

Gallo, Max. *The Night of Long Knives.* New York: Harper & Row, 1972.

Gay, Peter. *Weimar Culture.* New York: Harper & Row, 1968.

Gordon, Harold J. *Hitler and the Beer Hall Putsch.* Princeton, N.J.: Princeton University Press, 1972.

Grunberger, Richard. *The Twelve-Year Reich.* New York: Holt, Rinehart & Winston, 1971.

Grunfeld, Frederic V. *The Hitler File.* New York: Random House, 1974.

Hanser, Richard. *Putsch! How Hitler Made Revolution.* New York: P. H. Wyden, 1970.

Hitler, Adolf. *Mein Kampf.* New York: Reynal & Hitchcock, 1939.

————. *My New Order.* New York: Reynal & Hitchcock, 1941.

Holborn, Hajo. *Republic to Reich.* New York: Pantheon Books, 1972.

Kaplan, Chaim A. *Scroll of Agony.* New York: Macmillan, 1965.

Kelley, Douglas. *Twenty-two Cells in Nuremberg.* New York: Greenberg, 1965.

Klein, Burton H. *Germany's Economic Preparations for War.* Cambridge, Mass.: Harvard University Press, 1959.

Kohn, Hans. *The Mind of Germany.* New York: Scribner's, 1960.

Langer, C. Walter. *The Mind of Adolf Hitler.* New York: Basic Books, 1972.

Laqueur, Walter Z. *Weimar.* New York: Putnam's, 1974.

Lorant, Stefan. *Seig Heil!* New York: Norton, 1974.

Ludecke, Kurt G. W. *I Knew Hitler.* New York: Scribner's 1937.

Maltitz, Horst von. *The Evolution of Hitler's Germany.* New York: McGraw-Hill, 1973.

Manvell, Roger. *Goering.* New York: Simon & Schuster, 1962.

————. *The Hundred Days to Hitler.* New York: St. Martin's Press, 1974.

Maser, Werner. *Hitler: Legend, Myth, and Reality.* New York: Harper & Row, 1971.

Meyer, Henry C. *The Long Generation.* New York: Walker, 1973.

Mosse, George L. *Germans and Jews.* New York: H. Fertig, 1970.

————. *Nazi Culture.* New York: Grosset & Dunlap, 1966.

Musmanno, Michael A. *The Eichmann Kommandos.* London: Peter Davis, 1962.

Nicholls, Anthony J. *German Democracy and the Triumph of Hitler.* New York: St. Martin's Press, 1972.

Payne, Robert. *The Life and Death of Adolf Hitler.* New York: Praeger, 1973.

Phillips, Walter A. P. *The Tragedy of Nazi Germany.* New York: Praeger, 1969.

Picker, Henry. *Hitler Close Up.* New York: Macmillan, 1973.

Pope, Ernest R. *Munich Playground.* New York: Putnam's, 1941.

Rauschning, Hermann. *The Revolution of Nihilism.* New York: Longman, Green, 1939.

Ravenscroft, Trevor. *The Spear of Destiny.* New York: Putnam's, 1973.

Rosinski, Herbert. *The German Army.* New York: Praeger, 1966.

Schlabrendorff, Fabian von. *The Secret War Against Hitler.* New York: Pitman, 1965.

Schleunes, Karl A. *The Twisted Road to Auschwitz.* Urbana: University of Illinois Press, 1970.

Schoenbaum, David. *Hitler's Social Revolution.* Garden City, N.Y.: Doubleday, 1966.

Shepherd, Gordon. *The Anschluss.* Philadelphia: Lippincott, 1963.

Shirer, William L. *Berlin Diary.* New York: Knopf, 1941.

————. *The Rise and Fall of the Third Reich.* New York: Simon & Schuster, 1960.

Snyder, Louis L. *Encyclopedia of the Third Reich.* New York: McGraw-Hill, 1976.

Speer, Albert. *Inside the Third Reich.* New York: Macmillan, 1970.

Stein, George H. *Hitler.* Englewood Cliffs, N.J.: Prentice-Hall, 1968.

Steinert, Marlis G. *Twenty-three Days: The Final Collapse of Nazi Germany.* New York: Walker, 1969.

Stephenson, Jill. *Women in Nazi Society.* New York: Barnes & Noble Books, 1975.

Stern, Joseph P. *Hitler: The Fuhrer and the People.* Berkeley: University of California Press, 1975.

Strawson, John. *Hitler's Battles for Europe.* New York: Scribner's, 1971.

Toland, John. *Adolf Hitler.* Garden City, N.Y.: Doubleday, 1976.

Villard, Oswald G. *The German Phoenix.* New York: A. Smith and R. Haas, 1938.

Vogt, Hannah. *The Burden of Guilt.* New York: Oxford University Press, 1964.

Watt, Richard M. *The Kings Depart.* New York: Simon & Schuster, 1968.

Weiss, John. *Nazis and Fascists in Europe, 1918–45.* Chicago: Quadrangle Books, 1969.

Wheaton, Eliot B. *Prelude to Calamity.* Garden City, N.Y.: Doubleday, 1968.

Wheeler-Bennet, John W. *The Nemesis of Power.* New York: Macmillan, 1953.

Wulff, Wilhelm T. H. *Zodiac and Swastika.* New York: Coward, McCann, & Geoghegan, 1973.

INDEX